The Practical Forex Trader

Azhar ul Haque Sario

Copyright

Contents

Introduction

Chapter 1: What is Foreign Exchange and Why Does it Matter?

What is Foreign Exchange (Forex/FX)?

Think of foreign exchange (FX) as the giant swap meet where different countries' money gets traded. Just like you might trade your old baseball cards for a cool seashell, countries and businesses trade currencies to do, well...everything.

Why do we need Forex?

International Trade: Imagine a Pakistani company selling rugs to an American buyer. The Pakistani company wants rupees, and the American buyer has dollars. Forex is the marketplace where they can make that swap to get the deal done.

Travel: Heading to France? You'll need to swap your dollars or rupees for euros so you can buy croissants and museum tickets.

Global Investments: Big investors want a piece of the action all around the world. Forex lets them swap their home currency and invest in stocks, bonds, or hot new startups in other countries.

The Quirks of Forex
24/7 Market: Unlike your local shop, Forex never closes for the night. It's a worldwide, around-the-clock currency exchange party.

All About Pairs: In Forex, currencies are always traded in pairs – like US dollars vs. Japanese yen (USD/JPY) or euros vs. British pounds (EUR/GBP).

Tiny Changes, Big Money: Currency values wiggle by teensy-weensy amounts called "pips". But since giant sums of money change hands, those tiny moves can translate into huge profits (or losses).

Case Studies

The Vacationer: Sarah heads to Mexico. She converts $500 USD at an exchange rate of 20 Mexican pesos per dollar. She gets 10,000 pesos and has a blast on her trip.

The Import Business: A US company imports electronics from China, priced at 10,000 Chinese yuan (CNY). The current exchange rate is 6.5 CNY for every 1 USD. The company needs to pay roughly $1538 USD to their supplier.

The Wily Investor: Jim sees the Canadian dollar weakening against the US dollar. He bets $10,000 USD on this trend. If the Canadian dollar drops further, he could make a tidy profit by buying it back cheaply later on.

Sources

Investopedia Introduction to Forex
XE Currency Exchange: https://www.xe.com/

Important Note: Forex trading is awesome but can be super risky. Fluctuating currencies can mean big changes in your investment values, both up and down. Always do your homework before diving into the FX pool!

A Motley Crew of Players

The foreign exchange market (forex) is a sprawling global bazaar where currencies change hands at breakneck speed. It's not some stuffy, exclusive club – a surprisingly diverse cast of characters keeps this market humming. Let's dive into who these players are and peek behind the curtain of their forex dealings.

1. Big-Shot Banks: The Heavy Hitters

Think of banks as the heavyweights of the forex world. They're middlemen, essentially. Businesses, tourists, and investors need to swap currencies, and these banks make it happen. But it's not just a service – banks have their own skin in the game. They trade currencies for themselves, hoping to turn a tidy profit on exchange rate fluctuations.

Unusual Angle: Banks often have dedicated "prop desks" (short for proprietary trading). Picture a room full of traders glued to screens, betting the bank's own money on currency moves. Talk about high stakes!

2. Corporate Giants: Hedging Their Bets

Imagine a US-based car manufacturer selling loads of vehicles in Europe. They get paid in euros, but their bills are in dollars. Wild swings in exchange rates could seriously screw up their profits. That's where forex comes in – these companies use it to "hedge," or lock in favorable exchange rates to limit this risk.

Unusual Detail: Sometimes companies use exotic currency instruments called "derivatives." Sounds complex, but the idea's simple: it's like signing an insurance contract for currency risk.

3. Money Mavens: Investors and Funds

Think hedge funds, pension funds, the whole nine yards. These folks manage boatloads of cash and forex is an irresistible playground. Some play it safe, seeking steady returns. Others are pure speculators, betting big on currencies going up or down – think high-risk, potentially high-reward.

Case Study (Hypothetical): A Japanese pension fund worries about the yen weakening, which could hurt returns for retirees. They might buy US dollars in the forex market as a hedge. In essence, they're betting that even if the yen tanks, their dollar holdings will offset losses.

4. You and Me: The Retail Crowd

The forex market isn't just for the whales. Anyone with an internet connection and a bit of cash can trade currencies these days, thanks to online brokers. Some folks are day traders, trying to scalp quick profits from tiny price movements. Others are long-term players, riding currency trends over weeks or months.

Unusual Word Choice: Retail traders are sometimes likened to the "plankton" of the forex market – small, numerous, and often getting eaten by the bigger fish (institutions).

5. The Puppet Masters: Central Banks

Central banks, like the Federal Reserve in the US, are the true titans behind the scenes. Their job is to manage a country's economy, and one of their tools is influencing currency value. How? Sometimes they intervene directly in the forex market, buying or selling massive amounts of currency. Just the hint of their presence can send markets into a frenzy.

Numerical Case Study (Hypothetical): Japan's economy is sluggish. The Bank of Japan starts buying up US dollars with printed yen, flooding the market. This cheapens the yen relative to the dollar, aiming to make Japanese exports more attractive and boost growth.

Important Notes

Beware the Jargon Jungle: Forex is rife with terms like "pips," "carry trade," and "lots." Don't let it intimidate you – break it down piece by piece.
It's a 24/7 Circus: Unlike stock markets, forex never sleeps. Currencies trade nonstop, so something's always happening somewhere in the world.

Sources (Remember, always verify!)

Investopedia on Forex Participants: https://www.investopedia.com/articles/forex/11/who-trades-forex-and-why.asp
Corporate Use of Derivatives (a bit technical): [https://www.imf.org/external/pubs/ft/wp/2004/wp04177.pdf]

When the Currency Tango Gets Awkward

Imagine you're planning a trip to Europe. You've budgeted everything in your home currency, but those Euros you need keep changing their value! That's foreign exchange at work.

The Strong Currency Dance: Your currency buys more foreign goods and services – think fancy Parisian dinners or Spanish souvenirs that are suddenly a bit cheaper.

The Weak Currency Blues: Your money doesn't stretch as far. That dream trip now seems out of reach because hotels, meals, and even that cute little gondola ride all cost a lot more.

Case Study: Let's say 1 USD was equal to 0.90 Euros last year. Your €90 hotel room cost you a nice $100. This year, 1 USD only buys 0.75 Euros. That same hotel room? A hefty $120!

Unusual Angle: Think about the impact of FX fluctuations on locals. Picture a street vendor in Thailand. When their currency weakens against the US dollar, tourists flock to them (yay!), but it also means things they import, like those cool souvenirs they make, get more expensive (boo!).

Online Shopping: The World at Your Fingertips, But at What Price?

Online shopping makes those cute Korean skincare products or sleek Japanese gadgets oh-so-tempting. But those prices aren't set in stone!

The Bargain Hunter's Delight: Your currency is strong? That Japanese watch might be a steal! Foreign exchange rates might suddenly have you browsing international sites instead of local ones.

The "Whoops" Moment: Your currency tanks, and suddenly that "affordable" overseas purchase isn't so affordable after all. Remember those hidden fees too – foreign transaction fees, sneaky shipping costs...

Case Study: Your local store sells that fancy gadget for $200. But the Japanese site has it listed at 22,000 Yen. At a strong exchange rate (1 USD = 120 Yen), that's about $183! BUT factor in shipping, the chance your currency weakens while the package is in transit, and you could end up paying more.

Unusual Angle: Online shopping puts currency power (or lack of) in YOUR hands. A small business owner in a country with a weak currency might suddenly find their local products appealing to strong-currency customers seeking bargains.

International Investments: Where Risk and Reward Get a Global Spin

Investing abroad can be exciting, but FX throws in some curveballs:

The Sweet Spot: A strong home currency means your foreign investments grow even fatter when you convert profits back home. That 10% return in the UK stock market? Even sweeter with a favorable exchange rate.

The Bitter Pill: Your currency weakens, and those strong overseas returns shrink when brought back home. Your investment may have done great, but the currency exchange ate your gains.

Case Study: You invest $10,000 USD in a German company when 1 USD = 0.95 Euros. Your investment grows 15%! But now 1 USD = 0.80 Euros. While you made money, it's less in USD terms due to the exchange rate.

Unusual Angle: Sometimes the risk LIES in your home currency. A strong home currency might encourage investing locally. But what if your own currency suddenly tanks? Those "safe" returns aren't so safe anymore.

Important Notes:

Don't Panic Over Daily Fluctuations: FX markets change constantly - focus on long-term trends.
Watch Out For Fees: Banks, brokers, they all want a slice of your exchange pie. Compare services for the best deals.
Information is Power: Know the exchange rates before any transaction, and consider tools like hedging to manage risks in international investments.

Sources:

Investopedia on Foreign Exchange and the Individual: https://www.investopedia.com/articles/forex/053115/understand-indirect-effects-exchange-rates.asp
IAS Plus: Standard on Forex Effects: https://www.iasplus.com/en/standards/ias/ias21

The Not-So-Silent Shaper of Business

We hear "globalization" a lot, but what does it really mean for businesses? One huge factor is foreign exchange (FX or forex), the marketplace where currencies dance and change value against one another. It might seem like abstract finance-world stuff, but FX has sneaky ways of impacting your bottom line.

Import/Export: It's Not Just About Price Tags

Think of an American company importing toys from China. They pay in Chinese yuan, the seller gets paid in their own currency – everyone's happy, right? Now, imagine the US dollar suddenly weakens against the yuan. Those toys just got pricier for the importer, even if the yuan price stays the same. Ouch!

Flip the scenario. A US firm exports gadgets to Europe. If the euro strengthens against the dollar, suddenly those gadgets look more attractive to European buyers. Hello, sales boost! The key is that FX changes the relative cost of goods and services across borders, regardless of the "sticker price".

Numerical Case Study

Company A: Imports $1 million of materials from Mexico (assume an exchange rate of 20 Mexican pesos per US dollar).
FX Shift: The dollar weakens, now 25 pesos per dollar.
Impact: Same materials now cost $1.25 million, a 25% cost surge, even though the peso price stayed the same.

Supply Chains: A Web of Hidden Costs

Picture a car manufacturer. Sure, they deal with FX when buying steel from overseas, but it's deeper than that. Their overseas suppliers also have their OWN suppliers, who all use different currencies! FX ripples create a complex web of cost shifts. Even purely domestic companies can get hit if their domestic competitors use imported materials – the weaker dollar might make their prices soar.

Unusual Angle: Geopolitics Talk Through Currency

Wars, trade pacts, even elections – they don't just cause news headlines, they make currencies jump around. Let's say a major oil exporter faces supply disruptions. Even if your business doesn't touch oil, currencies tied to oil-heavy economies might get volatile. Suddenly, your costs when dealing with those countries become a gamble.

Hedging: The Insurance Policy Against Currency Chaos

Businesses hate uncertainty, so they use "hedging". Think of it as buying insurance against bad FX swings. Here are a couple of ways:

Forwards: Lock in an exchange rate today for a future transaction. Downside? You miss out if the rate moves in your favor by then.

Options: More flexible. Gives you the right, but not the obligation, to exchange currency at a set rate later. Costs upfront, though.

Numerical Case Study

Company B Expects a €1 million payment in 3 months. Worried the dollar will weaken vs. the euro.

Forward Hedge: Locks in a rate of $1.10 per €1.

Payoff: Even if the spot rate is $1.05 per €1 at the time, they STILL get their $1.1 million.

Unusual Word Choices

Instead of "impact" try "imprint" – it's subtler. "Global economy" is bland, how about "the interconnected marketplace"?

Sources (Remember, Always Verify!)

XE Currency Converter (For Live Exchange Rates): https://www.xe.com/

Investopedia: Guide to Hedging: https://www.investopedia.com/trading/hedging-beginners-guide/

Interesting Case Study on FX and Apple: https://www.studypool.com/documents/5760204/international-financial-management-apple

Its Global Sway

Foreign exchange (FX, or forex) is the marketplace where the world's currencies change hands. It's a bit like a giant dance floor where currencies waltz and tango, their values constantly shifting relative to one another. This dance has vast implications for the global economy, shaping trade and shaping the financial health of nations.

Trade Flows: The Currency Connection

Think of trade as a two-way street. When a country exports goods, it wants to get paid in a strong currency that will buy it lots of imports. Conversely, importers want to pay in a weaker currency to get better deals. Exchange rates play a huge role here.

Case Study: Let's say a US company exports cars worth $1 million to Japan. When the US dollar strengthens against the Japanese yen, suddenly those cars become more expensive for Japanese buyers. This could lead to less demand and hurt the American car exporter. On the flip side, Japanese electronics might look a lot cheaper to US consumers.

The trade equation isn't always straightforward. While weaker currencies can boost exports, they also make crucial imports like oil or manufacturing components more costly. This can lead to inflation and ultimately damage economic competitiveness.

Currency Stability: Bedrock or Quicksand?

Currencies, ideally, should be a stable unit of measurement for economic activity. However, FX markets are sometimes more like wild horses than tame workhorses. Here's where the unexpected angles come in:

Speculation: Forex is the largest market in the world, and a lot of that trading isn't about buying shirts made in China or selling coffee from Brazil. Speculators bet on currencies rising or falling, and their actions can sometimes cause excessive volatility. It's like adding a bunch of excitable partygoers to the currency dance floor – things can get a bit chaotic.

Geopolitical Tremors: Elections, wars, and natural disasters don't just send shockwaves through societies. They can make currencies shiver. Countries seen as safe havens often see their currencies strengthen in turbulent times, while those perceived as risky may see capital fleeing for stabler shores.

Numerical Case Study: The Swiss franc is often considered a safe-haven currency. During the 2008 financial crisis, investors flocked to the franc, driving its value up sharply. This had a ripple effect on the Swiss economy, making Swiss exports suddenly more expensive and hurting tourism industries dependent on foreign visitors.

What's the Upshot?

The impact of foreign exchange on the global economy is complex and far-reaching. Here are some key takeaways:

Interconnectedness: Forex acts like a web, tying together economies across the planet. A tremor in one place can be felt far away.

Trade Offs: There's rarely a "free lunch" in forex. A weak currency might be a boon to exporters, but it can sting importers and fuel inflation.

Importance of Stability: Wild currency swings are like sandstorms for economic planning. Businesses and investors prefer a degree of predictability.

Behind every exchange rate change, there are real people: exporters worried about losing sales, families facing pricier groceries, or investors scrambling to protect their wealth.

Sources (for reference and further research)

The Foreign Exchange Market (Investopedia): https://www.investopedia.com/terms/forex/f/foreign-exchange-markets.asp

Factors influencing exchange rates (Investopedia): https://www.investopedia.com/trading/factors-influence-exchange-rates/

Swiss Franc as a Safe Haven (Wikipedia)

Chapter 2: The Building Blocks of Currency Exchange

Beyond the Basics of Currency Pairs

We all get the gist of it – currencies get traded in pairs on the foreign exchange (forex) market. But the world of forex is a bit like an iceberg: you see the usual suspects above the water (major pairs), but there's a lot more lurking beneath. Let's dive a bit deeper.

Major Pairs: The Ol' Reliables

You know the drill: EUR/USD, USD/JPY, GBP/USD... the heavy hitters that make up most of the forex action. They're like blue-chip stocks: liquid, predictable (well, mostly), and always in demand. But they can get a bit...dull.

Think of major pairs like your favorite pair of jeans: comfortable, but not exactly going to spark a fashion revolution.

Minor Pairs: Spice Things Up

Minors (also called "crosses") are where it gets interesting. These pairs don't involve the USD. EUR/GBP, AUD/JPY – a little more off-the-beaten-path. Picture them as that pair of funky patterned pants you only bust out on special occasions. They've got potential for flair, but might also make you question your life choices if things go wrong.

Exotics: The Wild Frontier

This is where the real forex adventurers play. Exotics pair a major currency with one from an emerging market – think USD/ZAR (South African Rand) or EUR/TRY (Turkish Lira). It's the equivalent of trekking through uncharted jungles: high risk, potentially high reward, and the chance you might stumble across something truly unique.

Why the Obsession with Pairs?

It boils down to relativity. Currencies don't exist in a vacuum. When you buy EUR/USD, you're essentially betting that the Euro will get stronger relative to the US dollar. It's a constant tug-of-war.

Word Play: Forex Lingo Gets Weird

Forex traders have their own quirky lingo:

   "Cable": GBP/USD (from the old transatlantic cables used for quotes)
   "Fiber": EUR/USD (slang, no fancy history here)
   "Aussie": AUD/USD
   "Kiwi": NZD/USD

Don't be afraid to pepper these in for some insider cred.

Numerical Case Studies

Let's make this tangible:

Case 1: Minor Pair Volatility

Compare the average daily move (in pips) of EUR/USD to EUR/JPY over the past month. Is there a significant difference? Why might that be?

Case 2: Exotic Pair Adventure

Track the USD/BRL (Brazilian Real) over a turbulent period (find a significant economic or political event in Brazil's history). Can you spot the impact on the exchange rate?

Unusual Angles

The Psychology of Pips: A "pip" is the smallest price change in a pair. Explore how the tiny size of pips can warp a trader's psychology.
Geopolitics as Market Mover: Elections, trade wars – it all impacts currencies. Delve into a specific example of how a major political event rocked a currency pair.

Sources

These should get you started:

[https://www.babypips.com/learn/forex/buying-selling-currency-pairs
[Investopedia on Currency Pairs]([https://www.tradingview.com/]

The Quotable Exchange Rate

An exchange rate is basically a price tag for one currency in terms of another. You'll see it written like this:

EUR/USD 1.07

This means one Euro (EUR) will snag you 1.07 US dollars (USD).

The Bid-Ask Tango

Here's where things get a tiny bit trickier. Like buying a concert ticket, there are two prices you'll encounter:

Bid price: What a dealer will pay you for your currency.
Ask price: What a dealer will charge you to buy a currency.

The difference between the two is the "spread," and that's how dealers make their profit. Let's imagine you're swapping USD for Euros:

EUR/USD: 1.0650 / 1.0700
You'd get 1.0650 Euros for each USD you sell (bid price)
You'd need to pay 1.0700 USD to buy each Euro (ask price)

Why Do Exchange Rates Fluctuate?

Currencies aren't static. Their values bob up and down like boats on a choppy sea. These shifts are driven by a whole bunch of complex things:

Economics: Strong economy? Currency tends to be stronger (think jobs, trade, etc.)

Interest Rates: Higher interest rates on a currency can make it more attractive.

Politics: A wobbly government or new policies can make currencies nervous.

Plain old speculation: Traders bet on currencies just like stocks, influencing prices.

Case Study: The Traveling Coffee Bean

Let's say a US coffee roaster buys beans from Colombia. When the USD is strong against the Colombian Peso (COP), they get more beans for their buck. But, if the USD weakens, those beans get pricier. This directly impacts the price of your morning cup of joe.

Case Study: The Vacation Swap

You've saved up for a dream trip to Paris. A year ago, EUR/USD was 1.20. That swanky hotel room would have cost $100 a night. But now, the exchange rate is EUR/USD 1.05. Ouch, that same room just got more expensive!

Practical Tips

Shop around: Rates differ between banks, exchange bureaus, etc.

Watch the news: Big economic or political events can shake up FX rates.

Time it wisely: If you can, avoid exchanging currency at airports or tourist traps (they often have less favorable rates).

Consider FX risk: When doing international business, factor exchange rate fluctuations into your planning.

Unusual Words and Phrases to Spice Up Your Understanding

The FX waltz: Instead of "fluctuate," picture currencies waltzing to changing tempos.

Currency muscle: A strong currency has more "muscle" against others.

The whisper network: FX traders communicate and influence prices like a giant whisper network.

Sources

Investopedia on Exchange Rates:: https://www.investopedia.com/terms/e/exchangerate.asp

https://www.xe.com/: https://www.xe.com/

Pips and Spreads: The Hidden Costs of Forex Trading

At first glance, foreign exchange (or forex) trading can seem alluring. No commissions to worry about – sounds like a sweet deal, right? But the way forex brokers make their money is a bit sneakier, hidden within pips and spreads. Let's break down these sometimes-confusing concepts.

A Pip by Any Other Name...

Think of a pip as the tiniest possible price movement in a currency pair. It stands for "percentage in point" or sometimes "price interest point." For most pairs, one pip is 0.0001. So, if EUR/USD moves from 1.1051 to 1.1052, that's a one-pip change.

   Unusual Detail: Pips are different for currency pairs with the Japanese yen (JPY). Since JPY is less valuable, pips are measured to the second decimal place (like 120.40).

The Elusive Spread

Imagine you're in the market for a new phone. Store A sells it for $600, but Store B will buy it from you for $550. That $50 difference is like the spread in forex. Brokers give you two prices for a currency pair:

   Bid price: What they'll pay you for the base currency in the pair.
   Ask price: What you'll pay them to buy the base currency.

The tiny gap between these prices is where brokers make their profit.

Unusual Word Choice: Think of the spread as a "convenience tax." Instead of a set commission, you pay for the immediacy of executing your trades.

Case Study: The EUR/USD Spread in Action

Let's say the EUR/USD quote is 1.1051/1.1053.

You want to buy 100,000 Euros. That'll cost 100,000 x 1.1053 = $110,530 USD.
You immediately decide to sell. Oof! You'll only get 100,000 x 1.1051 = $110,510 USD back.
You just lost $20 to the spread!

How Spreads Impact Your Trading

Narrower spreads are generally better, meaning less cost to you. Factors affecting spread size include:

Liquidity: Popular currency pairs (majors like EUR/USD) tend to have tighter spreads.
Volatility: Spreads widen during crazy market swings, as brokers protect themselves against risk.
News events: Big announcements can shake things up, leading to wider spreads.

Unusual Angle: Think of the spread like paying for space on a crowded bus. On a packed bus (low liquidity), you might have to pay more for a seat. Same with forex!

Numerical Case Study: Comparing Spreads

Imagine you're considering these trades:

EUR/USD: Spread of 2 pips
GBP/NZD: Spread of 8 pips (less common pair)

Let's say you trade 100,000 units of each:

EUR/USD cost: 2 pips x $10/pip (standard lot) = $20
GBP/NZD cost: 8 pips x $10/pip = $80

The less-common pair ends up significantly more expensive!

Sources & Further exploration

BabyPips on Spreads:
https://www.babypips.com/learn/forex/what-is-a-spread-in-forex-trading
Investopedia on Pips:
https://www.investopedia.com/terms/p/pip.asp

Remember, this is just a jumping-off point! Consider exploring:

How do brokers make money beyond the spread?
Strategies for minimizing the impact of spreads on your trading.
The difference between fixed and variable spreads.

Types of Forex Orders: A Practical Guide with a Twist

Foreign exchange (forex) trading is a whirlwind of price fluctuations. To navigate this dynamic market, you must master different order types. Let's dive in and add a pinch of unexpected vocabulary to spice things up!

1. Market Orders: For the Impatient Trader

The Gist: A market order is like yelling "Buy!" or "Sell!" It's all about instant gratification.

When You'd Use It: You need to get in or out of the market quickly, and a few pips (tiny price changes) here or there don't really faze you.

Unusual Angle: Think of market orders like hailing a taxi during rush hour. You're guaranteed a ride, but the fare might be a bit unpredictable.

2. Limit Orders: Patience is a Virtue

The Gist: A limit order says, "I'll only buy/sell at this specific price or better." It's about exercising some control over your entry/exit.

When You'd Use It: When you have a target price in mind and are happy to wait until the market reaches that level.

Unusual Angle: Limit orders are like setting a price alert on your favorite online store. You won't buy those sneakers unless they dip below your desired price.

3. Stop-Loss Orders: Your Safety Net

The Gist: A stop-loss order is your insurance policy. It automatically closes your trade if the price moves against you by a certain amount, capping your losses.

When You'd Use It: Always. Seriously. Risk management is essential in forex.

Unusual Angle: Think of a stop-loss order as a parachute. It might not be the most comfortable way to exit, but it sure beats crashing and burning.

4. Stop-Entry Orders: The Ambush Predator

The Gist: A stop-entry order goes, "If the price breaks this level, I'm in!" It allows you to jump on trends or breakouts as they happen.

When You'd Use It: When you've spotted a potential move and want to pounce automatically if things heat up.

Unusual Angle: Stop-entry orders are like setting a mousetrap for a trend. You wait patiently until the market triggers it, and then SNAP!

Numerical Case Studies

Let's make this abstract stuff more tangible with some examples. Imagine you're trading the EUR/USD currency pair.

Case Study 1: Limit Order in Action

Current Price: EUR/USD = 1.0500

Your Target Buy Price: 1.0450 (You believe the euro will temporarily weaken.)

You place a BUY LIMIT order at 1.0450.

If the market drops to 1.0450, your order gets filled, and you're now long EUR/USD.

Case Study 2: Stop-Loss Saves the Day

You bought EUR/USD at 1.0500.
You place a STOP-LOSS order at 1.0400 (you're willing to risk 100 pips).
The euro unexpectedly plummets. Your stop-loss triggers at 1.0400, closing your trade and limiting your loss.

Beyond the Basics

The order types we've covered are like your forex toolbox essentials. But there's more! Here are a few extra tools for the savvy trader:

Trailing Stops: Automatically adjust your stop-loss as the market moves in your favor, locking in profits.
OCO (One Cancels the Other): Link a stop-loss and a take-profit (limit) order for total automation.

Sources (Remember, Always Verify!)

https://www.babypips.com/learn/forex/types-of-orders
Investopedia - Forex Orders

Introduction to Leverage and Margin in Foreign Exchange

In the realm of foreign exchange (forex) trading, leverage and margin are like a pair of high-octane roller skates. They can accelerate your journey, but if you're not careful, a spectacular wipeout might be in the cards.

Understanding Leverage: It's a Loan, Not Magic

Think of leverage as a loan you get from your forex broker. This loan allows you to control a much larger chunk of currency than you'd usually be able to with your own cash.

Example: With a leverage ratio of 100:1, a deposit of $1,000 lets you trade as if you had $100,000 at your disposal.

Leverage is tempting. It's the promise of amplifying your potential profits. But, like that extra-spicy vindaloo, it also amps up potential losses. It's the whole "high risk, high reward" gamble.

Margin: Your Good Faith Deposit

Margin is the money you put down as a kind of security deposit. It proves to your broker that you're serious about the trade and not going to run away if things go south.

Example: With a 2% margin requirement, to trade $100,000 worth of currency, you'd need a margin of $2,000 in your account.

Why the Hype? Low Barriers to Entry, Potential for Big Moves

Small Players, Big Dreams: Leverage is what attracts many traders to forex. You don't need a massive bankroll to play with the big boys (and girls).

Small Moves, Big Impact: Currency pairs often move in tiny fractions. Leverage lets you turn those seemingly insignificant fluctuations into potentially noteworthy gains (or losses).

The Catch: Not for the Faint of Heart

Leverage is a volatile beast. Here's why:

Magnified Mistakes: Just as gains get amplified, so do losses. If the market moves against you, you can lose more than you initially invested.

Margin Call: The Dreaded Knock: If your losses eat into your margin deposit too much, the broker will issue a "margin call." This means you either cough up more cash or your positions get closed automatically (usually at the worst possible moment).

Numerical Case Studies

Scenario 1: When Things Go Right

Investment: $500
Leverage: 50:1
Controlled Position: $25,000 worth of EUR/USD
Market Move: EUR appreciates by 1% against USD
Gain: $250 (without leverage, it would've been a measly $5)

Scenario 2: Ouch, That Hurts

   Same investment, leverage, and position as Scenario 1
   Market Move: EUR depreciates by 1% against USD
   Loss: $250 (your initial investment could be
significantly reduced, or worse, wiped out).

Unusual Angles to Consider

   Psychology of Leverage: It can make traders
overconfident, leading to reckless decisions. It's tempting
to think you're invincible with a leveraged account.

   The "Overnight Fee": Holding leveraged positions
overnight usually incurs fees. This eats away at potential
profits.

Sources

   [Leverage in Forex Trading]
(https://www.investopedia.com/articles/forex/07/forex
_leverage.asp)
   [Margin Explained]
(https://www.babypips.com/learn/forex/leverage-
defined)

Important Note: This is just a primer. Forex trading is
inherently risky, and leverage adds another layer of
danger. Thorough education and calculated risk
management are absolutely crucial.

Chapter 3: A Brief History of Foreign Exchange Markets

Barter Systems and Early Currencies

The modern financial world is a labyrinth of stock exchanges, crypto-transactions, and complex derivatives. Yet, the bedrock of all these systems lies in the humble beginnings of barter and the earliest forms of currency. Let's dive into this evolution, unearthing peculiarities and the practical wisdom behind these archaic systems.

Bartering: The Original "Marketplace"

Before coins clinked in pockets, the barter system reigned supreme. Its premise was beguilingly simple – a swap of one good or service for another. A Neolithic farmer might trade a bushel of grain for a clay pot, or a skilled cobbler might barter a pair of sandals for a night's lodging.

Oddball Currencies

The barter system had its limits, which ignited the need for a standardized medium of exchange. Here's where things get quirky:

Massive Stones: On the island of Yap, gargantuan limestone discs called Rai stones functioned as currency. The larger the stone, the greater its value. Oddly, moving them wasn't necessary – simple ownership transfer sufficed.

Salt: In ancient Rome, salt was worth its weight in gold. Roman soldiers were sometimes paid in this precious seasoning, giving rise to the word "salary" (from the Latin 'salarium').

Seashells: Cowrie shells, with their glossy finish, were a widespread currency in Africa, Asia, and even parts of the Americas. Their portability and relative scarcity made them valuable trade tokens.

Numerical Case Study: The Inefficiencies of Barter

Imagine a village with a farmer, a potter, a blacksmith, and a weaver. The farmer needs pots, the potter needs tools, the blacksmith needs cloth, and the weaver needs grain. In a pure barter system:

Each person must find someone who directly desires the goods/services they offer.

'Fair value' is subjective. How many eggs equal a haircut? Haggling ensues.

Goods are perishable. A surplus of apples is worthless if you can't trade them quickly.

The Birth of Coinage: Practicality Prevails

The drawbacks of barter spurred the birth of coinage. Precious metals like gold and silver were ideal: durable, divisible, and universally valued. Stamped coins guaranteed weight and purity, streamlining transactions.

Lydia's Breakthrough: Around the 7th century BCE, the kingdom of Lydia (modern-day Turkey) likely pioneered the concept of standardized coinage. This innovation fueled trade and economic expansion.

Case Study: Coinage vs. Barter

Suppose a farmer has a surplus of 50 bushels of wheat they want to exchange for a horse.

Barter: Finding a horse-owner needing that exact quantity of wheat is difficult and time-consuming.
Coinage: The farmer sells the wheat for coins, then confidently shops for a horse, knowing the coins hold accepted value for all horse sellers.

Beyond the Obvious: Barter's Modern Relevance

While barter seems like a relic of the past, it persists in surprising ways:

Corporate Barter: Companies sometimes exchange surplus goods or services, facilitating transactions that would be difficult with cash alone.
Skill-Swap Communities: Websites and apps allow individuals to barter skills like babysitting, language lessons, or handyman services.
Crisis Situations: In economic downturns, some people turn to barter networks to obtain essentials when currency systems are disrupted.

Sources

[The History of Money: From Barter to Banknotes] (https://www.investopedia.com/articles/07/roots_of_money.asp)
[Unusual Forms of Currency] ([invalid URL removed])
Barter Systems: [https://www.investopedia.com/terms/b/barter.asp

Remember: Unusual Doesn't Equal Impractical

This exploration shows that while early financial systems seem primitive compared to today's markets, they were born of necessity and real-world problem-solving. Sometimes, looking back at these oddball currencies and barter systems offers unexpectedly practical wisdom.

Understanding the Gold Standard

Simple Definition: A monetary system where a country's currency held a fixed value against a set quantity of gold. The government guaranteed to redeem its currency for that gold on demand.

Historical Context: The gold standard was widely adopted in the late 19th and early 20th centuries, providing currency stability. It eventually fell out of favor in the 20th century, primarily due to economic shocks and the constraints it placed on governments.

Mechanics: A country on the gold standard had to maintain sufficient gold reserves to back all its issued currency. This created a theoretical limit to the amount of money they could print.

Angles to Explore

Uncommon Word Choice: Consider using words like "specie" (referring to gold or silver coins) or phrases like "convertibility" and "fixed parity" to give your writing a more technical, authoritative feel.

The Gold Standard as a Straitjacket: Focus on the limitations it placed on governments during economic crises. They couldn't simply print more money to stimulate the economy, and they had to defend the fixed exchange rate of their currency against speculators.

Gold Standard Nostalgia: There's a degree of romanticism about the gold standard. Why does this persist, even though economists widely agree it's impractical today? What psychological appeal does it hold?

Numerical Case Studies

The Great Depression: Many blame the severity of the Depression on countries clinging to the gold standard. You could research how deflationary pressures were intensified because governments were limited in their economic response options.

Bretton Woods System: After WWII, a modified gold standard was adopted (only the US dollar was directly convertible to gold). Investigate how this system worked and why it collapsed in the 1970s.

Hypothetical Gold Standard Today: What would it take for a modern economy to adopt the gold standard again? Play around with calculations about the gold price, and how much a government would have to hoard to make this feasible.

Unexpected Details

"Barbarous Relic": John Maynard Keynes' famous description of the gold standard still resonates. Why did a brilliant economist have such disdain for it?

Counterintuitive Effects: Ironically, while aimed at stability, the gold standard might have worsened some economic crises. Explore how the need to adjust to gold inflows/outflows created additional volatility.

The Wizard of Oz Connection: Some believe L. Frank Baum's book was a political allegory about the gold standard vs. free silver debates of the late 19th century.

World Gold Council: The Classical Gold Standard:
https://www.gold.org/history-gold/the-classical-gold-standard
Federal Reserve History: Gold Standard
Investopedia: Gold Standard
https://www.investopedia.com/terms/g/goldstandard.asp

The Bretton Woods System

In the wake of World War II's economic devastation, the 1944 Bretton Woods Agreement sought to stabilize a fractured global economy. Think of it as the world's nations huddled together, blueprints in hand, trying to rebuild a shattered financial house. The core idea: let's peg currencies to the US dollar and let the dollar hold the ultimate anchor – gold itself.

The Rules of the Game

Goldilocks Currencies: Nations agreed to keep their currencies from veering too far up or down against the dollar – like Goldilocks, they needed a "just right" exchange rate. Central banks had to intervene to keep their currencies in a narrow band.

America's Golden Promise: The US, flush with gold reserves, pledged to keep the dollar's worth steady at $35 per ounce of gold. It sounded reliable – the dollar was, metaphorically, "as good as gold."

The IMF: Financial Firefighter: The Bretton Woods system spawned the International Monetary Fund (IMF). Its job? Lend money to countries facing balance of payment problems, ensuring the system wouldn't seize up.

Why Bother?

The architects of Bretton Woods wanted to escape the chaotic, beggar-thy-neighbor currency policies of the 1930s. Unstable currencies made business riskier and discouraged global trade. This system offered a bit more certainty, potentially boosting commerce.

The System in Action: A Numerical Case Study

Imagine you're a French cheese exporter in 1955. Bretton Woods means you know, with relative certainty, how many US dollars your delicious Camembert will fetch across the Atlantic. Let's say:

Agreed Exchange Rate: 1 US Dollar = 350 French Francs
Your Cheese Price in France: 1000 Francs

With a stable exchange rate, you calculate the US price as roughly $2.86 (1000 Francs / 350 Francs/Dollar = $2.86). Sure, there were tiny fluctuations allowed, but the big currency swings were supposed to be a thing of the past.

The Cracks Appear

The Bretton Woods system worked reasonably well... for a while. But cracks started to show:

America's Gold Dilemma: As the US printed more dollars to fund programs like the Vietnam War, other nations got nervous. Could America really honor the promise to exchange all those dollars for gold at $35 an ounce? Trust began to wane.

Stubborn Imbalances: Countries with chronic trade surpluses (like West Germany) saw their currencies get stronger. Under Bretton Woods rules, they theoretically should have adjusted their economies to weaken their currencies. They often resisted, leading to tensions within the system.

The System Crumbles

By the early 1970s, faith in the dollar was in tatters. Countries holding big dollar reserves demanded gold, betting the US couldn't keep its promise. President Nixon hit the panic button in 1971, suspending the dollar's direct convertibility to gold, effectively shattering the foundation of Bretton Woods.

The Unexpected Legacy

Free-Floating…Mostly: Today most major currencies float, meaning governments don't rigidly defend a specific exchange rate. But Bretton Woods was hardly a waste of time. Central banks still watch exchange rates like hawks; it's just that they have more tools at their disposal than before.

The IMF Lives On: The IMF endures but in a transformed role. It's no longer about defending the dollar-gold system but more about crisis lending and monitoring global economic health.

Unusual Details to Spice Up Your Writing

Not So Shiny Agreement: The phrase "Bretton Woods" sounds grand, but the actual agreement took only three weeks to hammer out in the scenic New Hampshire resort town. World-changing deals can sometimes come together in a hurry.

Keynes the Contrarian: Famed economist John Maynard Keynes had his own, more flexible, plan for the post-war order. His ideas lost out to a system valuing the perceived certainty of gold.

Sources

IMF Archives: [invalid URL removed]
Federal Reserve History:
https://www.federalreservehistory.org/essays/bretton-woods-created

The Rise of Floating Exchange Rates

In the realm of international finance, the way currencies are valued against one another has undergone a fundamental shift. Gone are the days of rigid exchange rates, meticulously pegged to gold or other stable assets. Now, a system known as "floating exchange rates" dominates the scene, where currency values dance and sway in response to the ever-shifting tides of global markets.

A Brief History Lesson

Before the widespread adoption of floating exchange rates, systems like the Bretton Woods agreement or the gold standard held sway. These systems aimed for stability by fixing a country's currency value to a specific, agreed-upon commodity. The trouble was, real-world economic forces often strained these pegs, leading to crises, devaluations, and the need for drastic adjustments.

By the 1970s, the Bretton Woods system was crumbling under the strain of economic growth and imbalances. This paved the way for the widespread adoption of floating exchange rates – a system where markets largely determine the worth of one currency relative to another.

How Floating Exchange Rates Actually Work

Picture a bustling marketplace filled with currencies from around the globe. Instead of a shopkeeper setting fixed prices, imagine forces of supply and demand dictating the value of each currency:

Demand is Key: If investors, businesses, and everyday people desire a particular currency, its value climbs. Think of a hot new product everyone wants – the price naturally rises.

Supply Matters: If a country floods the market with its currency, its value tends to drop. Too many of anything usually makes its price go down.

Economic Health Check: A country with robust economic growth, low inflation, and a sound fiscal policy generally sees its currency appreciate. It's like having a product with a strong reputation.

And Don't Forget Speculation: Traders constantly bet on which currencies will rise or fall in the short term, adding an element of volatility.

Numerical Case Study: The Euro's Fluctuations

Let's look at a concrete example: the Euro. Since its creation in 1999, the euro has been a floating currency against others like the US dollar. This means its value can change daily.

Hypothetical Scenario: Suppose a positive economic report about the Eurozone is published. Increased investor confidence leads to more demand for euros. As a result, the euro's value might rise from 1 euro = 1.10 US dollars to 1 euro = 1.20 US dollars.

Unexpected Angles and Unusual Details

The Geopolitical Factor: International events, even those seemingly unrelated to markets, can send shockwaves through exchange rates. Elections, conflicts, or natural disasters can trigger sudden shifts in how currencies are valued.

The "Carry Trade" Conundrum: Savvy investors sometimes borrow in low-interest-rate currencies and then invest in higher-interest-rate countries. This practice, called the carry trade, can put upward or downward pressure on certain currencies, further adding to the mix.

Pros and Cons of Floating Exchange Rates

This system isn't perfect. Here's a balanced look:

Pros

Self-Adjustment: Floating rates help a country's balance of payments adjust more naturally. Deficits or surpluses tend to correct themselves over time through currency movements.

Monetary Policy Freedom: Countries have greater independence in setting interest rates and managing their own economies.

Shock Absorber: Floating rates can cushion the blow of external economic shocks.

Cons

Volatility: This can be disruptive for businesses and traders who need predictability.

Speculation: Excessive speculation can lead to exaggerated currency swings that don't reflect underlying economic fundamentals.

Competitive Devaluations: A temptation exists for countries to deliberately weaken their currency to gain a trade advantage, potentially sparking trade tensions.

The 20th Century: A World of Shifting Standards

The Gold Standard Era (pre-WWI): Currencies were pegged to a fixed amount of gold, leading to relatively stable exchange rates. Think of it like every country's currency was a differently colored poker chip, all redeemable for the same weight in gold.

Numerical Example: $20.67 could get you one ounce of gold, and that indirectly fixed the British pound to the US dollar.

Interwar Chaos (1918-1939): The gold standard was abandoned during WWI. Post-war attempts to return to gold floundered. Currencies floated freely, leading to wildly unpredictable exchange rates.

Unexpected Angle: This volatility made international trade a gamble! Imagine ordering German goods in January, but the value of the mark collapses by the time you have to pay in April.

Bretton Woods (1944-1971): To restore stability, a new system emerged. The US dollar was pegged to gold, and other currencies were pegged to the dollar. Currencies were only allowed to fluctuate within a narrow band.

Word Choice Twist: Think of the US dollar as the "anchor currency" in this era.

The Collapse of Bretton Woods (1971-1973): The US faced pressure to print more dollars than it had gold to back up. President Nixon took the dollar off the gold standard, allowing for floating exchange rates we're still familiar with today.The 21st Century: Technology and Turmoil

The Rise of the Euro (1999): A significant event! Many European countries adopted a single currency, creating a massive economic bloc and a major rival to the US dollar. This simplified trade within Europe but created fluctuations between the euro and other global currencies.

Electronic Trading Revolution: Gone were the days of shouting traders on phone lines. Online platforms allowed lightning-fast trades, accessible to big institutions and even individual investors.
Numerical Example: Trades that took minutes now happen in milliseconds, making forex a high-speed, volatile game.

The 2008 Financial Crisis and Beyond: Major disruptions sent shockwaves through the forex market. Central banks took unconventional actions like quantitative easing, which impacted currency values.
Unexpected Angle: Safe-haven currencies, like the Swiss franc or the Japanese yen, sometimes spiked in value when investors got nervous.

Unusual Details and Case Studies to Explore:

"Carry Trades": Investors borrowed in low-interest-rate currencies (like the Japanese yen for a long time) and invested in high-yield currencies. This worked great...until it didn't! Look into the 2008 crisis and the impact on carry trades.
Emerging Market Currencies: Not just about the dollar, euro, and yen anymore. Currencies like the Brazilian real or the Indian rupee are growing influential, but often exhibit more volatility.

The "Flash Crash" of 2010: A still-debated event where the British pound plummeted temporarily due to algorithmic trading gone awry. Highlights the risks of automation.

Sources (Remember to double-check these!):

Bank for International Settlements - Forex historical data: https://www.bis.org/
Federal Reserve History- Bretton Woods: [invalid URL removed]
Investopedia for unusual terms like "carry trade": https://www.investopedia.com/

Section I: Understanding the Fundamentals

Chapter 4: Economic Factors Driving Exchange Rates

Interest Rates & Currency Demand

Introduction

The foreign exchange (Forex) market isn't just about charts and flashing numbers. It's a complex dance driven by global economic forces, and interest rates are the maestros conducting the orchestra. A shift in interest rates in one country relative to another creates ripples of change that can boost or batter a currency's value.

The Basics: How Interest Rates Shape Currency Demand

The Allure of High Yields: Investors, like savvy shoppers, hunt for the best returns. When a country raises interest rates, its currency becomes a hotter commodity. Picture this: higher interest rates mean bigger payouts on bonds and deposits, drawing investors who need to exchange their currency to buy these assets. Increased demand buoys the currency's value.

The "Carry Trade" Conundrum: This strategy exploits interest rate differences between countries. Investors borrow in low-interest-rate currencies and invest in high-interest-rate ones. The profit? Pocketing the difference. This can fuel massive currency flows, but it's a fickle mistress – sudden interest rate shifts can unwind these trades, sending currencies tumbling.

Case Study: The US Dollar's Dominance

Let's look at the mighty US dollar. In 2022, the Federal Reserve cranked up interest rates to combat scorching inflation. Result? A surge in the dollar's value. Why? Investors flocked to US assets for higher returns. But this had consequences:

Emerging Markets Mayhem: Countries with dollar-denominated debts suffered. A stronger dollar made it costlier to repay loans, straining their economies.

Export Pain: US goods became pricier for foreign buyers, potentially hurting American exporters.

Beyond the Obvious: Factors that Muddle the Waters

It's not a perfect science! Here's why interest rate changes don't always dictate currency movements:

Inflation Expectations: If a high-interest-rate country is also grappling with runaway inflation, its currency may not be that appealing. Investors worry that rising prices will eat into their returns.

Economic Outlook: If a country hikes rates but investors foresee a gloomy economic future, the currency could tank. It's not just about the rate, but the confidence in the underlying economy.

"Safe Havens" in Times of Trouble: During turmoil, investors ditch riskier currencies in favor of 'safe havens' like the Japanese yen or Swiss franc, often regardless of interest rates.

Case Study: The Curious Case of Japan

Japan is a fascinating anomaly. Despite near-zero interest rates for decades, the yen has sometimes strengthened. How? Factors like Japan's hefty overseas investments and reputation as a safe harbor outweighed the low-interest rate factor.

Words Matter: Nuances in Terminology

Let's get a bit word-nerdy to avoid generic writing:

"Relative" Interest Rates: Stop focusing on rates in isolation! It's the difference between countries that drives currency flows.

"Real" vs. "Nominal" Rates: Inflation bites. Investors care about 'real' returns – interest rates adjusted for inflation.

"Risk Premium:" Higher interest rates may signal economic instability. Investors might demand extra compensation (a risk premium) reflected in currency prices.

Sources for Further Exploration

[Investopedia on Interest Rates & Currencies] (https://www.investopedia.com/ask/answers/040315/how-do-changes-national-interest-rates-affect-currencys-value-and-exchange-rate.asp)

IMF Blog: Interest Rate Differentials and Exchange Rates

Inflation, the Exchange Rate Phantom, and the Disappearing Value of Money

We often treat money like it's rock-solid. A dollar is a dollar, right? Yet, inflation, that sneaky economic phantom, quietly erodes the stuff in our wallets. Prices creep up, and suddenly our cash buys a little less. This dance between inflation and purchasing power forms the heart of a critical concept: purchasing power parity (PPP).

The Basket of Goods: More Than Just Groceries

Picture this: you take a basket and fill it with everyday items - bread, petrol, a movie ticket. This same basket costs $100 in the US. Now, imagine flying to Japan. Could you buy the exact same basket for the equivalent of $100 in Yen? Probably not, and that's where PPP and exchange rates get interesting.

PPP: The Great Equalizer

Purchasing power parity tries to level the playing field. It's a theory saying that, over time, the real exchange rate between currencies should adjust so that our hypothetical basket of goods costs roughly the same in any country, once we've converted the prices.

Why does this matter? Picture an undervalued currency. Let's say, hypothetically, our basket of goods becomes super cheap in Mexico compared to the US. In theory, this creates an arbitrage opportunity – traders could swoop in, buy cheap Mexican goods, and sell them at higher US prices. This demand pushes the Mexican peso up, making their goods more expensive again until the gap, in theory, closes. Of course, the real world is messy - transport costs, tariffs, and market imperfections mean PPP is a guiding principle, not an iron law.

Case Study: The Big Mac Index

The Economist magazine playfully illustrates PPP with their "Big Mac Index". They compare how much a Big Mac costs globally, converting prices into dollars. In theory, a Big Mac should cost about the same everywhere, right? The deviations from PPP that the index reveals can hint at whether currencies are overvalued or undervalued.

Example: If a Big Mac costs $5 in the US, and a theoretically equivalent one costs $3 (converted to dollars) in Argentina, this suggests the Argentine Peso might be undervalued against the dollar.

Inflation's Bite: A Real-World Tale

Let's make this less abstract. Say the US experiences higher inflation than Japan. American products become relatively more expensive. In PPP terms, you'd expect the dollar to weaken against the yen to compensate. Why? Because to keep our "basket of goods" at price parity, Japanese products need to be relatively cheaper when converted to dollars.

Numerical Example:

Year 1: 1 USD = 100 Yen. A $10 US t-shirt is the same price as a 1000 Yen Japanese t-shirt.

Year 2: US inflation surges by 10%, but Japan's stays low. The US t-shirt now costs $11.

PPP Suggests: To maintain parity, perhaps the new exchange rate should be something like 1 USD = 90 Yen . Now, the Japanese shirt, still 1000 Yen, feels cheaper for Americans (~ $11.11), restoring balance.

Beyond the Textbook: PPP's Wrinkles

Like any economic model, PPP has its limitations:

Not All Goods Are Equal: Traded goods (cars, electronics) conform to PPP better than non-traded stuff (haircuts, restaurant meals). Local costs matter!

Quality Matters: Is a Japanese t-shirt exactly like the US one? PPP assumes perfect substitutes, which rarely exist.

"Sticky" Prices: Exchange rates can adjust way faster than the price of goods in shops. PPP is a long-term trend, not a daily market arbiter.

The Bottom Line for Traders and Travelers

FX Traders: PPP is one factor among many driving exchange rates. It offers a long-term view, not short-term trading signals.

Businesses: Where are inputs cheapest, and where's the most buying power for your sales? PPP concepts influence global business decisions.

Travelers: That cheap-looking destination may be less of a bargain once your strong home currency is converted under an unfavorable exchange rate.

Sources

Investopedia: Purchasing Power Parity (PPP)
The Economist: The Big Mac Index:
https://www.economist.com/big-mac-index

GDP: The Quirky Yardstick of Economic Success

When we talk about a country's economic health, the phrase Gross Domestic Product (GDP) gets tossed around like confetti at a New Year's bash. But what exactly is this magical number, and does it really tell us if a country's getting richer or poorer?

Let's get down to the nitty-gritty. Think of it like a giant shopping receipt for a nation – it includes everything from fancy smartphones and haircuts to military tanks and bridge repairs.

The GDP Roller Coaster: Understanding Growth

If a country's GDP increases, we generally assume that its economy is growing. After all, more stuff is being produced and sold, right? But, just like a roller coaster, GDP can have its ups and downs.

A recession is like the plunge down the roller coaster's steep drop– GDP shrinks for a while, businesses struggle, and people might lose their jobs. On the flip side, an economic expansion is that exhilarating uphill climb – GDP grows, businesses flourish, and things are generally looking rosier.

The Foreign Exchange Factor: GDP's Fickle Friend

A nation's GDP has a complicated love-hate relationship with foreign exchange rates (how much your currency is worth relative to others). Let's look at a couple of scenarios:

Scenario #1: Strong Currency, Weaker Exports

Imagine your country's currency is like a muscle-bound superhero. When it's stronger relative to other currencies, your imports become cheaper – yay for bargain-hunting! But your exports become more expensive to foreign buyers. This can potentially drag down your GDP growth if exports are a big chunk of your economy.

Scenario #2: Weaker Currency, Export Boost

On the other hand, if your currency takes a hit and becomes weaker, it works like a discount coupon for your exports. Foreign buyers get more bang for their buck, potentially leading to an increase in exports. This could give your GDP a nice little boost.

Case Study Time!

Let's add some numbers to make this abstract stuff more concrete:

Japan: The Export Powerhouse

Japan is heavily reliant on exports. Over the years, the Japanese yen has had its ups and downs versus currencies like the US dollar. A weaker yen makes Japanese cars, electronics, etc., more attractive to global buyers, potentially contributing to GDP growth. [Source: You'll need a reputable economic analysis source for specifics]

Venezuela: Currency Crisis and Spiraling GDP

Venezuela's economic woes are complex, but a big part of the problem has been the collapse of its currency, the bolívar. With a severely devalued currency, imports become incredibly expensive, leading to shortages and skyrocketing inflation. This wreaks havoc on GDP. [Source: Look for news articles/analyses on Venezuela's economic situation]

GDP: Not a Crystal Ball

GDP is a mighty important indicator, make no mistake. But it's not perfect. Here's why:

The Blind Eye: It doesn't account for things like quality of life, income distribution, environmental damage, or the unpaid work that keeps societies running.
The "Underground" Economy: Shady or informal economic activities aren't captured in GDP figures.

In the End...

GDP is a bit like a fickle friend- useful, but needs to be taken with a grain of salt. For a fuller picture of a country's economic well-being, we need to look at it alongside other indicators. Think of GDP as one piece of a larger, fascinating economic puzzle.

Understanding the Balance of Trade

At its core, the balance of trade (BOT) reflects the difference between what a country sells to other countries (exports) and what it buys from them (imports).

Trade Surplus: Exports exceed imports... hooray, positive balance!
Trade Deficit: Imports exceed exports... time for some trade strategy adjustments.

Why Does BOT Matter?

The balance of trade isn't just about numbers; it has real-world implications:

Economic Growth: A trade surplus can boost a country's economy, fueling domestic industries and job creation.
Currency Value: Exchange rates can fluctuate with the BOT. Countries with persistent deficits might see their currency weaken against those with surpluses.
Global Interdependence: In our interconnected world, one country's trade imbalance affects its trading partners.

Unusual Angles to Explore

Now, let's steer clear of the typical BOT discussion and inject some unexpected details:

The Hidden Trade: Services, such as banking, tourism, and software development, are increasingly part of the global trade picture. How does the "invisible trade" of services impact the conventional BOT?
Beyond Goods: Ideas, intellectual property, and cultural products also cross borders. How does the intangible exchange of assets and influence factor into a

nation's economic well-being, potentially offsetting traditional trade imbalances?

The Environmental Angle: Does a country's BOT reflect where the true costs lie? Countries exporting heavily polluting goods might look good on paper, but the long-term environmental and social costs challenge the rosy picture.

Word Choice for Impact

Let's avoid bland phrasing with a touch of unexpected vocabulary:

Instead of "trade flows," consider "currents of commerce."

Replace "trade deficit" with the more vivid "trade chasm."

Instead of "economic growth," try "economic vitality."

Numerical Case Studies

Let's make things tangible with some examples (please note: these are illustrative, be sure to research the latest figures).

Germany, the Export Powerhouse: Germany's precision engineering and manufactured goods have consistently created a trade surplus. However, its reliance on imported energy reveals a potential vulnerability in the BOT.

The US-China Trade Relationship: The complex interplay between these economic giants heavily influences global trade. Explore the specific products and sectors driving the often-contentious imbalances.

A Small Nation's Big Success: Countries like Singapore, specializing in specific niche areas (e.g., technology, financial services), can achieve strong trade surpluses despite limited resources.

Advanced AI Assistance

Here's how AI can further elevate your writing:

Trend Analysis: AI-powered tools can analyze vast amounts of trade data to reveal subtle shifts or patterns invisible to the naked eye.
Unconventional Connections: AI might suggest unexpected links between the balance of trade and factors like political stability or climate change.
Predictive Modeling: Explore AI models to consider potential future scenarios for trade imbalances and their potential economic consequences.

Source Links (Illustrative - Please Verify)

World Trade Organization: https://www.wto.org/
International Monetary Fund: https://www.imf.org/en/Home
World Bank Data: https://data.worldbank.org/

Government Debt, Budget Deficits, and the Dance of Foreign Exchange

Governments, like many of us, sometimes find themselves spending more than they earn. This gap between expenditures and revenue is known as a budget deficit. When deficits persist, they accumulate into a hefty pile known as government debt. While domestic economic impacts are well-trodden territory, the relationship between government debt, deficits, and foreign exchange rates (FX) is a more nuanced waltz.

The Mechanics

Interest Rates: To fund deficits, governments borrow money by issuing bonds. Rising debt often leads to higher interest rates to entice lenders. These higher rates can attract foreign investors seeking better returns. This surge in foreign capital strengthens a country's currency on the FX market.

Inflation: Excessive government borrowing to cover deficits can fuel inflation if it overheats the economy. Inflation erodes a currency's purchasing power, making it less attractive in the eyes of international investors, leading to a potential decline in its FX value.

Confidence Crisis: If investors get spooked by unsustainable levels of debt or a reckless fiscal policy, they might ditch a country's bonds en masse. This "capital flight" would create a deluge of sell orders for that nation's currency, weakening its FX value.

Unusual Angles

The Safe Haven Paradox: Ironically, currencies of countries with traditionally safe and stable economies (think the US dollar or Japanese yen) sometimes benefit from increased government debt. Investors, fearing instability elsewhere, flock to these "safe haven" currencies, paradoxically boosting them even amidst fiscal imbalances.

Geopolitical Debt: Debts owed to foreign nations aren't just a financial issue; they become leverage in international relations. A heavily indebted nation might feel pressured to adjust its foreign policy to appease its creditors.

The Currency Wars: Sometimes, countries might deliberately try to weaken their currencies through increased debt or deficit spending. A weaker currency makes exports cheaper, boosting competitiveness, though at the risk of imported inflation.

Numerical Case Studies

Japan: Debt Giant, Currency Darling: Japan has one of the world's highest debt-to-GDP ratios, yet the yen remains a strong currency. This illustrates the safe-haven effect and Japan's unique economic structure. [Source: https://en.wikipedia.org/wiki/National_debt_of_Japan]

Venezuela: Inflation and FX Collapse: Venezuela's hyperinflation fueled by reckless deficits, demolished the bolivar's value. Citizens turned to foreign currencies, creating a black market for FX. [Source: https://en.wikipedia.org/wiki/Hyperinflation_in_Venezuela]

The 1997 Asian Financial Crisis: This crisis was partly triggered by unsustainable debt in Southeast Asian nations. Foreign investors pulled out, currencies crashed, and the economic fallout was severe. [Source: https://simple.wikipedia.org/wiki/1997_Asian_financial__crisis]

Word Play (avoid these in final writing, but they might spark ideas)

The Fiscal Tango: Government financial decisions aren't solo performances; they're an intricate dance with foreign exchange markets.

Borrowing Boomerang: Debt taken on today can come back to hit a nation's currency value in the future.

Investor Mood Swings: Foreign exchange isn't just about numbers; it's influenced by the fickle sentiment of global investors.

Important Notes

FX markets are incredibly complex – this is a simplified overview!

Country-specific contexts matter immensely; generalizations are dangerous.

Consider exploring the debate on whether deficits even matter in the long run.

Chapter 5: Central Banks: The Power Players in Forex

The Central Banks

Central banks, like the Federal Reserve (the Fed), the European Central Bank (ECB), and the Bank of Japan (BoJ), are unique beasts in the world of finance. They're not your corner store bank – they're the powerhouses behind the curtain, steering nations' economies. Let's dissect their role, particularly how they shake things up in the wild world of foreign exchange (FX).

1. The Price Police: Keeping Inflation in Check

Think of central banks as the referees of inflation – keeping prices from spiraling out of control or, conversely, stagnating in a deflationary slump. Their primary weapon? Interest rates.

   Hike Time: When inflation gets too feisty (think 5% price climbs instead of the typical 2%), central banks often increase interest rates. This makes borrowing more expensive, discouraging spending and investment, which slows the economy and hopefully cools down inflation.

   Loosening the Reins: If prices are stubbornly low, central banks might slash interest rates. This cheapens borrowing, fueling spending and investment, hoping to give the economy a caffeine jolt.

Case Study: In 2022, the Fed aggressively raised interest rates from near 0% to over 4% to fight runaway inflation. This strengthened the US dollar in the FX market, as investors sought higher returns.

2. The Liquidity Lifeguard

Banks, like any business, need cash flow. Central banks act as the "lender of last resort," pumping money into the system when banks are short. This keeps the financial gears greased and prevents a total meltdown during crises.

Unusual Angle: During the 2008 financial crisis, central banks went further than ever. They bailed out banks and even bought up dodgy assets like mortgage-backed securities, actions that were unheard of just years before.

3. Money Maestros: Managing the Currency

Central banks are deeply intertwined with foreign exchange markets. This is where currencies are bought and sold, determining how many euros you get for your dollars. Central banks can try to influence these exchange rates. How?

Verbal Judo: Sometimes, the mere hint of future interest rate changes by a central bank can send its currency soaring or sinking in FX markets. We call this "jawboning."

Heavy Artillery: In rarer instances, central banks directly intervene in FX markets, buying or selling their currency to force a shift in its value.

Case Study: The Bank of Japan has repeatedly intervened to weaken the Japanese yen in recent years, trying to make Japanese exports more competitive.

4. The Economic Oracles

Okay, they don't have crystal balls, but central banks constantly analyze economic data. They release forecasts, reports, and hold press conferences, all of which are parsed by FX traders like ancient prophecies. Why? Because these signals give crucial clues about where a central bank might be heading with its policies.

Unusual Word Choice: Think of FX traders as hyperactive meerkats, constantly scanning the horizon for signals from central banks that might impact currency prices.

Beyond the Basics

The above are foundational roles, but central banks are evolving:

Climate Crusaders? Some, like the ECB, are exploring how to use their power to combat climate change, potentially favoring green investments.

Digital Currency Pioneers: Central banks are researching their own digital versions of cash ("central bank digital currencies"). This could totally reshape payment systems.

Let's Get Numerical
A 1% Fed interest rate hike can potentially translate into significant shifts in the USD/EUR exchange rate over time.
During volatile times, even a central bank tweet can cause sudden, sharp movements in FX markets.

Sources

Federal Reserve: https://www.federalreserve.gov/
European Central Bank:
https://www.ecb.europa.eu/home/html/index.en.html
Bank of Japan: https://www.boj.or.jp/en/index.htm/

Monetary Policy: Steering Foreign Exchange Markets

Introduction

Monetary policy is like the intricate workings of a ship's rudder, used by central banks to guide economies through the choppy seas of inflation, growth, and currency fluctuations. In the realm of foreign exchange (forex), monetary policy tools act as powerful levers, influencing the value of currencies and shaping global trade.

Core Monetary Policy Tools

Interest Rates: The Benchmark Tool

Think of interest rates as the 'price of money'. This can cool down an overheating economy by slowing down spending and investment, and it also tends to attract foreign investors seeking higher returns. A stronger currency due to higher interest rates can make a country's exports less competitive, impacting trade flows.
Case Study: Suppose the US Federal Reserve raises interest rates. This could strengthen the US dollar against the Japanese yen, making Japanese goods cheaper for Americans and potentially increasing US imports from Japan.

Open Market Operations (OMOs): Buying and Selling Power

OMOs are like a central bank's foray into the bond market. To inject money into the economy, a central bank buys government bonds, essentially pumping cash into the financial system. This can lower interest rates and make borrowing easier. Conversely, to tighten the money supply, a central bank sells bonds, soaking up excess cash.

Case Study: The Bank of Japan embarks on OMOs, buying Japanese government bonds. This could weaken the yen, making Japanese exports more competitive.

Quantitative Easing (QE): The Unconventional Weapon

QE is a relatively newer, more dramatic tool. It involves large-scale purchases of not just government bonds but also other financial assets like mortgage-backed securities. This floods the economy with money, driving down long-term interest rates and encouraging lending beyond what traditional OMOs can achieve.

Case Study: During the 2008 financial crisis, the US Federal Reserve used QE extensively. This helped lower mortgage rates and arguably supported the housing market's recovery.

Unusual Angles and Word Choices

The Signaling Effect: Beyond the direct impact on interest rates, central bank announcements, and even hints in their meeting minutes, can send powerful signals to forex markets. Use words like "vigilance' or "hawkish stance" to describe a central bank's potential to fight inflation with rate hikes.

Safe-Haven Currencies: In times of economic uncertainty, investors flock towards currencies perceived as stable, like the Japanese yen or the Swiss franc. This can occur even if interest rates in those countries are low. The phrase "flight to safety" emphasizes the psychological dimension of forex.

Carry Trade: A riskier strategy, this involves borrowing in a low-interest-rate currency and investing in a higher-yielding one. Changes in interest rate differentials can make carry trades very profitable or lead to major losses, adding volatility to forex.

Advanced AI Applications

Sentiment Analysis: AI-powered tools can analyze news articles, social media, and other textual data to gauge the overall mood regarding a currency. This can provide insights beyond traditional economic indicators.

Algorithmic Trading: AI algorithms are heavily used in forex, executing trades based on complex rules and historical patterns. Understanding algorithmic trading is crucial for analyzing forex market behavior.

Sources

International Monetary Fund (IMF): https://www.imf.org/en/Home
Bank for International Settlements (BIS): https://www.bis.org/
Financial Times: https://www.ft.com/

Central Bank Shenanigans in Forex Markets

Central banks, the enigmatic figures of the financial world, have a peculiar habit of dipping their toes into the vast ocean of foreign exchange markets. We call this "foreign exchange intervention," but you could think of it as a bit of currency market manipulation. Let's delve into why central banks do this, how it works, and the sometimes surprising consequences.

Why Central Banks Get "Handsy" with Forex

Taming the Exchange Rate Beast: Currencies can be volatile creatures, prone to wild swings in value. Central banks sometimes try to smooth out these bumps, especially if instability starts messing with their economic goals. A plunging currency, for example, can make imports a nightmare, fueling inflation.

The Export Advantage: Some countries rely heavily on exports. A weaker domestic currency can make their goods cheaper for foreign buyers, boosting sales. A central bank might try to nudge its currency lower to gain this competitive edge.

Bulking Up Reserves: Central banks hold stockpiles of foreign currency, like gold for a pirate. This serves as a rainy-day fund of sorts. Sometimes, they might intervene in the forex market to plump up their reserves.

The Tools of the Trade

Central banks don't just shout at the forex market to behave. Here's what they actually do:

Buying and Selling Spree: The most straightforward tactic. A central bank wanting to prop up its own currency will buy it on the forex market, using its foreign currency reserves. Want the currency to weaken? They sell a bunch of it.

The Power of Words: Sometimes, just talking about potential intervention can do the trick. Traders get nervous, and the market reacts as the central bank desires, even without it lifting a finger. Economists lovingly call this "jawboning".

Interest Rate Tinkering: This is a more indirect play. Raising interest rates can attract foreign investors, boosting demand for a currency and pushing its value up.

Messy Consequences: Beware the Unintended Side Effects

Forex intervention isn't a magic wand. It can have ripple effects that cause trouble:

The Speculator Strikes Back: Central banks are big, but forex markets are huge. Traders betting against a central bank can sometimes overwhelm their efforts, leading to losses and embarrassment.

Inflation Woes: A weaker currency might aid exports, but it hurts your buying power for imported goods. This price pressure can lead to inflation headaches.

Angry Neighbors: Countries don't exist in a vacuum. If everyone starts weakening their currencies to gain a trade advantage, it turns into a "race to the bottom" that benefits no one. This can lead to trade tensions and even "currency wars".

Numerical Case Studies

Let's make this more concrete:

Japan's Yen Worries (2022): The Japanese yen took a nosedive, causing economic concern. The Bank of Japan intervened, spending a reported $20 billion USD to prop the yen back up.

Switzerland's Franc Fight (2011): The Swiss franc, a safe-haven currency, was soaring in value. This was crushing Swiss exporters. The Swiss National Bank imposed a ceiling on the franc, requiring massive intervention to maintain it.

Central Bank Communications

Central banks are the towering figures of the financial world. Their words and actions reverberate through markets, sending currencies soaring or plunging. But for all their power, there's an often overlooked quirkiness to their communications – especially when it comes to foreign exchange markets. Let's explore some unexpected angles:

1. The Language of Ambiguity

Central bankers aren't your average conversationalists. They wield a unique language of deliberate ambiguity. It sounds strange, but there are reasons for this:

Maintaining Flexibility: The economic landscape shifts rapidly. Central banks need wiggle room to adjust policy without looking like they're flip-flopping. A slightly vague statement now can save face later.

Managing Expectations: Markets overreact. Carefully crafted ambiguity can nudge expectations in a desired direction without causing wild swings in currency values.

Case Study: Let's say a central bank hints at "possible near-term adjustments" to interest rates. Traders go into a frenzy. Is this a signal of a hike? A cut? The bank hasn't committed either way, but the market starts pricing in some kind of change.

2. Code Words and Market Folklore

The world of FX trading is steeped in its own jargon and lore. Central bankers have their own version. Certain words and phrases take on heightened significance, becoming market shorthand:

"Dovish": Signals a leaning towards looser monetary policy (lower interest rates), often causing a currency to weaken.

"Hawkish": The opposite, implying a tightening bias and potentially boosting the currency.

"Data-dependent": A classic non-committal phrase, indicating decisions will hinge on future economic indicators.

Case Study: Historically, some central bank governors have been notorious for triggering knee-jerk market reactions with specific phrases they were known to use. This becomes self-reinforcing market folklore.

3. The Power of Silence

Sometimes, what central banks don't say speaks volumes. Prolonged silences can be just as impactful as a surprise announcement.

Strategic Silence: A central bank may go quiet to signal satisfaction with the current policy stance or to avoid fueling speculation during a sensitive period.

Uncertainty: Silence can also reflect genuine internal uncertainty. This in itself sends a market signal – that things are less predictable than usual.

Case Study: Imagine a currency is under pressure, and the usual channels of central bank commentary dry up. Traders may interpret this as a sign that policymakers are either deeply concerned and unsure how to react or that an intervention is being planned behind the scenes.

4. When Central Banks Collide – Conflicting Signals

In a globally interconnected FX market, central banks don't operate in isolation. Their actions and words can create ripple effects and sometimes outright clashes with the signals from other major central banks.

Currency Wars: Not literal wars, but the term highlights tensions that arise when one central bank's actions make another country's currency uncomfortably strong, potentially hurting its exports.
Competing Narratives: Central banks might offer differing outlooks on global growth, leading to whipsaw effects in currencies as traders try to figure out who to believe.

Case Study: The US Federal Reserve raises rates, making the dollar stronger. This puts pressure on the European Central Bank who might feel compelled to follow suit, even if it's not ideal for their economy.

5. Oops! Central Bank Miscommunications

Even the most carefully calibrated messaging can backfire. Central bankers are human, and slip-ups happen. These can become legendary market mishaps.

The Misheard Word: A simple misspeaking or mistranslation can trigger wild market swings before the mistake is clarified.
Accidental Leaks: Premature hints at policy changes can send shockwaves through markets, even if unintentional.

Lost in Translation: Nuances of language can be misinterpreted, especially when speeches cross cultural and linguistic barriers.

Chapter 6: Geopolitics and Global Events

Political Stability and Its Impact on Currencies

In the realm of foreign exchange (FX), we often cling to the mantra of "political stability equals a strong currency". While this holds some truth, it's a simplification that obscures the fascinating nuances within this relationship. Let's delve into some unexpected angles and unusual details to spice up your analysis.

Not All Stability is Created Equal

The Iron Fist: A seemingly stable country ruled by an authoritarian regime might show currency strength initially. Yet this strength sits on shaky foundations. Suppressed dissent, opaque economic policies, and the looming threat of upheaval can create a ticking time bomb for investors.

The Fickle Democracy: A young democracy with frequent changes in leadership, while perhaps turbulent on the surface, often signals flexibility. It suggests an ability to adapt, correct course, and demonstrate resilience. In the long run, this may be more appealing to investors than a stagnant autocracy.

The Perception Game

Foreign exchange markets function largely on perception. Sometimes, the appearance of stability matters more than the reality. Here's where unusual word choices can add a unique perspective:

The Facade of Tranquility: A nation might carefully curate an image of order, masking simmering social discontent or unsustainable economic practices. Investors may initially be lulled, but savvy traders will look for cracks in the facade.

The Rumor Mill: FX markets are notoriously sensitive to hearsay. Whispers of a coup, brewing policy changes, or hidden corruption can trigger more significant volatility than the events themselves, should they ever occur.

Case Study: The Surging...Peso?

Let's imagine a fictional Latin American country, traditionally plagued by political instability. Let's call it "Mirador". Despite its history, Mirador sees a surprising surge in its currency. Why?

Rare Earth Windfall: Major deposits of critical minerals are discovered. This attracts global attention, overshadowing short-term political concerns.
The "Strongman" Appeal: A charismatic populist leader takes power, promising sweeping reforms and an end to corruption. While risky, some investors see this as a gamble signaling a potential break from past dysfunction.
Regional Power Shift: Mirador's more volatile neighbors plunge into deeper crises. By comparison, even modest instability in Mirador appears attractive.

Beyond the Headline Numbers: Indicators to Watch

Standard economic metrics alone won't tell the whole story. Keep an eye on:

Capital Flight: Are wealthy citizens or corporations rapidly moving assets out of the country? This can be a red flag regardless of official stability claims. [Source: Investopedia on Capital Flight: https://www.investopedia.com/terms/c/capitalflight.asp]

Black Market Exchange Rates: A large discrepancy between official exchange rates and black market rates signals distrust in the formal system. [Source: Council on Foreign Relations: [invalid URL removed]]

Social Media Sentiment: Advanced AI tools can analyze social media chatter in the native language to gauge true public sentiment. This can reveal the undercurrents of a society that government pronouncements obscure.

The Uncomfortable Truth

Sometimes, mild instability can have a paradoxically positive effect on a currency. Why?

The Hedge Appeal: When major global currencies are in turmoil, investors seek safe havens, even if those havens are 'less bad' rather than 'completely good'.

Betting on Change: A country with acknowledged problems may signal potential for significant reform. Investors may bet on a turnaround story before it becomes mainstream news.

Focus

Unusual angles: Emphasis on how uncertainty caused by trade wars impacts markets alongside the direct effects of tariffs.

Unexpected details: How smaller players in the global economy can be disproportionately impacted.

Unusual word choices: Where possible, to avoid typical phrasing.

Trade Wars: Volatility as the New Constant

Trade wars – when nations volley tariffs and trade restrictions back and forth – aren't new. But their modern-day frequency and the speed at which they escalate add a fresh layer of complexity for businesses navigating foreign exchange markets. The direct effect of tariffs is simple: the price of targeted goods increases in the importing country. The uncertainty arising from these conflicts, however, has more nuanced and far-reaching consequences.

Uncertainty as the Invisible Tariff

Investors and markets fundamentally dislike uncertainty. When tariffs are announced, businesses scramble to assess the fallout:

Supply Chains in Flux: Will input costs rise for domestic manufacturers, forcing price increases? Who are potential alternative suppliers, and at what cost?

Who's the Next Target? Fears that a trade war will spread to other goods or nations create a chilling effect on investment and spending.

The Rules are Changing: Uncertainty about future tariffs or regulations hampers long-term business planning.

This uncertainty breeds volatility. Exchange rates gyrate based not only on actual trade flows, but on rumors, threats, and speculation about the next round of escalation

Case Study: The Unseen Victims

Let's consider the US-China trade war's impact on Vietnam. Here's where numerical analysis can punch up your writing:

Apparent Winner: Vietnam saw a surge in exports to the US as companies sought to dodge China tariffs. Perhaps they saw a 20% year-on-year growth.

Deeper Dive: But, much of this was "pass-through." Chinese parts were assembled in Vietnam and labeled "Made in Vietnam." This has limited benefit to the Vietnamese economy.

Currency Risk: The flood of US dollars into Vietnam risks inflating their own currency (the dong), making their other exports less competitive.

This illustrates that the fallout is complex and disproportionate – a great point to flesh out in your writing.

Foreign Exchange – Riding the Rollercoaster

Here's how the dynamics of trade wars directly impact forex:

Safe Havens: Uncertainty drives investors to currencies like the US dollar, Swiss franc, or Japanese yen, appreciating them against others.

Exporter Woes: Countries with significant trade exposure to warring nations see their currencies weaken as export prospects dim.

Betting on the Future: Speculators take positions on currencies based on their views of how the trade war will play out, furthering volatility.

Navigating the Choppy Waters

Businesses caught in the crossfire need strategies, but it's like building a boat in a hurricane:

Scenario Planning: Not sexy, but vital. What if your key supplier's nation suddenly faces tariffs?

Hedging: Complex, but forex hedging tools can lock in rates, providing some insulation.

Agility is Queen: The ability to source new materials or shift production locations quickly becomes a strategic advantage.

Important Note: It is NOT the AI's place to forecast exchange rates. That's dangerously speculative. Instead, we're emphasizing the volatility created by these conflicts.

Sources (Remember, double-check these before using):

Reuters: Vietnam's Trade Boom Masks Old Problems: https://www.reuters.com/world/vietnam-exporters-fret-over-potential-trade-fallout-us-rules-xinjiang-2023-02-14/

Council on Foreign Relations: Trade Wars and Currency Wars: https://www.federalregister.gov/topics/foreign-currencies

Elections and Foreign Exchange: Navigating Policy Shifts

Elections inherently carry the potential for policy change. When a new government takes power, shifts in economic strategies and priorities can send ripples through financial markets, especially the volatile world of foreign exchange. Understanding these dynamics is crucial for businesses, investors, and anyone exposed to currency fluctuations.

Why Elections Matter to Forex

Fiscal Policy: Elected officials often campaign on promises related to taxation, spending, and debt management. These fiscal policies directly influence a nation's economic health, impacting its currency's attractiveness relative to others.

Monetary Policy: Central banks, while often independent, are still influenced by the political climate. Changes in interest rates, inflation targets, and money supply can profoundly affect a currency's value.

Trade Policy: Protectionist stances, tariffs, or the renegotiation of trade deals instigated by a new government can significantly swing a country's trade balance and, consequently, its currency.

Market Sentiment: Elections breed uncertainty. Traders and investors may react preemptively based on perceived risks or potential rewards associated with a new government, leading to forex volatility even before concrete policy changes occur.

Unexpected Angles

Coalition Governments: When no single party wins decisively, coalition governments may form. These often necessitate compromises, potentially diluting radical policy shifts and injecting more uncertainty into forex markets.

Minority Governments: A less powerful minority government might struggle to pass major legislation, creating prolonged policy limbo and currency instability.

Populist Movements: The rise of populist leaders, often campaigning on anti-establishment or nationalist platforms, can create significant market anxiety due to the unpredictability of their economic agendas.

Numerical Case Studies

Brexit (2016): The British pound (GBP) plummeted as the "Leave" campaign gained momentum, reflecting fears of economic disruption. The GBP/USD exchange rate fell over 10% in the immediate aftermath of the referendum.

U.S. Presidential Elections (2016): The unexpected victory of Donald Trump led to a surge in the US dollar (USD) based on anticipated tax cuts and infrastructure spending. However, his protectionist trade rhetoric contributed to ongoing volatility.

Emerging Markets: Elections in developing nations can have outsized effects on their currencies. A change in leadership may signal a shift towards greater economic stability (or instability), significantly impacting investor confidence and forex flows.

Unusual Word Choices

Bellwether: Certain elections or even specific regions within a country may be forex bellwethers, where early results hint at broader market reaction to policy shifts.

Temperamental: Currencies of nations with a history of political volatility could be described as having a temperamental nature in relation to elections.

Gyrations: Rather than saying a currency "fluctuated," consider describing "wild gyrations" during election periods.

Sources

IMF: Fiscal Policy and Elections (https://www.elibrary.imf.org/view/book/97814755479 00/ch003.xml)
World Bank: The Impact of Elections on Foreign Exchange Markets (Please note: I couldn't find a World Bank study specifically on this, but they likely have relevant data on political risk)
Financial Times / Wall Street Journal: Search their archives for case studies of specific elections and their impact on forex.

International Conflicts, Sanctions & Their Impact on Foreign Exchange

International conflicts and the economic sanctions that often accompany them send shockwaves through global markets, with foreign exchange (forex) markets being particularly sensitive.

The Basics

Sanctions: The Tools of Economic Pressure Economic sanctions are restrictions imposed by one country (or group of countries) on another to coerce changes in behavior. Sanctions take many forms:
Trade embargoes
Asset freezes (individuals, companies, or governments)
Restrictions on financial transactions
Travel bans

Forex Markets: Where Currencies Collide Forex markets are where currencies are traded against each other. Exchange rates are not stagnant; they fluctuate based on economic health, political stability, interest rates, and international events.

Key Impacts of Conflicts and Sanctions on Forex

Heightened Uncertainty and Volatility
International conflicts fundamentally introduce instability. Markets dislike uncertainty, leading to increased volatility in currencies associated with affected countries.
Example: Russia's 2022 invasion of Ukraine sent ripples through the forex market. The Russian ruble saw sharp declines, while 'safe-haven' currencies like the US dollar strengthened.

Disrupted Supply Chains and Trade Flows

Wars and major sanctions disrupt trade routes and production. This alters the supply and demand for goods and services denominated in particular currencies, impacting their value.

Case Study: Sanctions on Iran's oil exports have limited the availability of Iranian rials on forex markets, affecting its exchange rate.

Capital Flight and Shifting Investments

Investors in countries facing conflicts or severe sanctions often seek to move their assets into safer, more stable currencies. This 'capital flight' weakens the affected country's currency and strengthens those seen as safe havens.

Domino Effects on Neighboring Economies

Conflicts rarely stay confined. Neighboring countries may experience trade disruptions, refugee flows, and increased security costs. Their currencies may suffer along with the directly involved nations.

Example: The Syrian civil war's economic impact spread to neighbors like Lebanon and Jordan, putting pressure on their currencies.

Numerically Speaking: Case Studies

Ukraine (2022): The ruble (RUB) depreciated by roughly 50% against the US dollar (USD) in the immediate aftermath of Russia's invasion. However, the RUB has since recovered somewhat, likely due to Russia's capital controls and energy revenue.

Iran (2012, 2018): Sanctions targeting Iran's oil sector and access to the SWIFT financial system severely impacted the Iranian rial (IRR). The IRR lost significant value, leading to hyperinflation.

Unusual Angles to Consider

Black vs. Official Exchange Markets: In countries with strict currency controls due to sanctions or conflict, a black market for foreign exchange often exists. These black market rates can wildly differ from official rates, reflecting the true economic pressures.

Sanctions as Double-Edged Swords: While intended to punish, sanctions can have unintended consequences on the sanctioning nations. Losing access to commodities or markets may disrupt supply chains and drive higher prices globally.

The Rise of 'Weaponized Interdependence': Sanctions were once seen as tools of the strong against the weak. Now, interconnectedness means sanctions sometimes cause mutual damage, making them less clear-cut as a foreign policy tool.

Sources

The Impact of Sanctions on Exchange Rates: https://cepr.org/voxeu/columns/sanctions-and-exchange-rate)

The Effects of War on Exchange Rates: https://www.imf.org/external/np/fin/data/param_rms_mth.aspx

The Impact of Financial Sanctions: https://www.piie.com/research/trade-investment/sanctions

Section II: Tools and Techniques for Analysis

Chapter 7: Fundamental Analysis: Digging into Economic Data

Understanding Economic Forecasts: A Foreign Exchange Lens

Economic forecasts attempt to predict the future health and direction of economies. Think of them as weather predictions for financial markets. While never certain, these forecasts are crucial for businesses, investors, and governments, especially when dealing with foreign exchange (FX).

Why FX Matters

Foreign exchange markets determine the relative values of currencies around the globe. A vacation in Europe costs more when the dollar is weak against the euro – that's FX in action! Businesses trading internationally constantly manage FX risk. Economic forecasts directly impact FX markets for several reasons:

Interest Rates: Central banks set interest rates, a key economic indicator. Higher interest rates typically attract investors, strengthening a currency. Forecasts about interest rate changes can send currencies soaring or plummeting.

Inflation: Inflation means goods and services get more expensive over time. High inflation erodes a currency's value. Forecasts signaling rising inflation often lead investors to dump that currency.

Overall Economic Health: Forecasts about GDP (an economy's output), unemployment, and other indicators influence a currency's long-term strength. A healthy economic outlook boosts confidence in a currency.

Case Study: The Surging Dollar (Hypothetical)

Let's imagine a scenario. Major economic forecasts predict the US will outperform other developed economies in the coming year. Here's what could happen in FX markets:

Demand for Dollars Rises: Investors anticipate higher returns from US assets due to the strong forecast, so they want more dollars.

The Dollar Appreciates: Increased demand pushes the dollar's value higher against the euro, yen, and other currencies.

US Exports Get Pricier: A strong dollar makes American goods more expensive for foreign buyers, potentially hurting US exporters.

Winners and Losers: Multinational companies with significant overseas earnings would benefit as those foreign profits convert to more dollars. However, importers of foreign goods could face higher costs.

The Unpredictability Factor

Economic forecasts are like educated guesses. Here's where things get interesting (and where you can add unique angles to your writing):

"Black Swan" Events: Geopolitical shocks, wars, natural disasters, or even tweets from influential figures can torpedo the most careful economic forecasts.

Forecasters Are Human Too: Economic forecasting is part science, part art. Analysts bring their biases and blind spots to the table, even with the best of intentions.

The Butterfly Effect: Economies are complex systems. Tiny changes in one variable can create cascading effects that are hard to predict beforehand.

Unusual Details to Explore

Behavioral Economics: Economic forecasts try to predict how rational people should behave. In reality, humans are emotional. Research "herd mentality" and how it impacts FX markets during uncertainty.
Gaming the Forecasts: Do governments or large institutions ever try to manipulate economic forecasts in their favor? This could be a fascinating angle to explore.
The Language of Forecasts: Pay attention to the wording used in economic reports. Words like "may," "could," or "likely" signal varying degrees of certainty.

Sources for Further Investigation

International Monetary Fund (IMF) World Economic Outlook: https://www.imf.org/en/Publications/WEO
FocusEconomics: https://www.focus-economics.com/
Trading Economics: https://tradingeconomics.com/
Central bank websites (e.g., US Federal Reserve, European Central Bank)

Macroeconomic Themes and the FX Frenzy

The world of foreign exchange (FX) is a whirlwind of economic forces, where currencies dance to the tune of growth, recession, and interest rates. Understanding these macroeconomic themes is like having a compass in a stormy sea – without it, you're bound to capsize in the volatile FX market.

Growth vs. Recession: A Currency Tug-of-War

Picture the economy as a massive engine. When it's humming along (growth), investors feel optimistic. This optimism often leads to increased demand for a country's currency, as investors look to park their funds in thriving markets. A booming economy can fuel currency appreciation.

But when the engine sputters (recession), the mood turns sour. Investors get the jitters and scramble for safe havens. This 'flight to safety' frequently means ditching riskier currencies in favor of stalwarts like the US dollar. A recession can cause a currency to plummet.

Case Study: The Yen's Rollercoaster

Japan's economic stagnation in the 1990s, the "Lost Decade," turned the yen from a darling to a dud. On the flip side, China's meteoric rise in the early 2000s made the yuan a hot commodity.

Numerical Example:
   If the U.S. economy booms with 5% annual growth, the US dollar might appreciate 3% against a basket of currencies.

Conversely, a 2% contraction in the Eurozone economy could lead to a 4% decline in the euro.

Interest Rates: The Magnet for Money

Interest rates are the price of money. When central banks raise rates, it gets costlier to borrow. This attracts investors seeking higher returns. Currencies of countries with rising interest rates tend to strengthen, all else being equal.

Conversely, when rates fall, investors may seek greener pastures elsewhere, weakening a currency. Think of interest rates as a powerful magnet either pulling money in or pushing it out, impacting currency values in the process.

Case Study: The Carry Trade Conundrum

The "carry trade" is a classic FX strategy. Investors borrow in low-interest-rate currencies (like the Japanese Yen for years) and invest in high-yielding ones (think the Australian dollar at times). This works...until it doesn't. When global sentiment sours, the carry trade unwinds violently, with traders rushing to repay those low-yielding loans, causing those currencies to skyrocket.

Numerical Example:

If Australia hikes rates to 5% while Japan keeps them at 0%, the Australian dollar could surge against the yen.

A sudden rate cut by the Reserve Bank of New Zealand could cause the Kiwi dollar to crater.

Beyond the Basics: The Unusual Suspects

While growth and interest rates are kingpins, other factors lurk in the shadows, ready to shake up the FX world:

Geopolitics: Wars, sanctions, and elections can spark wild currency swings. Think about the Russian ruble's recent volatility.

Commodity Craze: Countries heavily reliant on commodity exports (think Australia with iron ore) see their currencies swayed by the whims of global commodity markets.

The "Whisper Number": Market expectations often trump reality. If economic data is weaker than the 'whisper number' (unofficial forecast), a currency can tumble even during growth.

The Bottom Line

The FX market is a complex beast, a tapestry woven with macroeconomic threads. Understanding these themes won't guarantee you trading profits, but it'll sure prevent you from getting blindsided by the next currency tremor.

Sector-Specific Analysis: Unraveling Currency Dynamics

In the realm of foreign exchange (FX), currencies are not monolithic entities. Their movements are often swayed by the ebb and flow of specific economic sectors. Understanding these sector-driven influences can be a potent tool for traders, investors, and policymakers seeking to navigate the ever-shifting FX landscape.

1. The Resourceful Realm: Commodities and Currencies

Nations rich in natural resources often see their currencies tethered to the cyclical nature of commodity markets. Let's consider these examples:

   Australia (AUD): A significant exporter of iron ore and coal, the Aussie dollar tends to appreciate during commodity booms, fueled by heightened demand from countries like China. Conversely, a downturn in commodity prices can pressure the AUD downward.
   Canada (CAD): The "Loonie" is frequently labeled a petrocurrency due to Canada's substantial oil exports. Rising oil prices generally bolster the CAD, while declines have the opposite effect.
   Norway (NOK): Similarly tied to oil, the Norwegian krone often mirrors the trajectory of oil prices.

Numerical Case Study: When oil prices soared in 2022, both the CAD and NOK outperformed many other developed market currencies. This underscores the potent link between resource wealth and currency strength.

2. Manufacturing Might: Exports and Exchange Rates

Countries with robust manufacturing sectors rely heavily on exports. Their currencies become intertwined with the competitiveness of their manufactured goods on the global stage.

Japan (JPY): A leading exporter of automobiles and electronics, Japan has historically benefited from a weaker yen, as it makes Japanese products relatively cheaper for foreign buyers. However, prolonged periods of yen weakness can fuel inflation and erode purchasing power.

Germany (EUR): The euro, while influenced by the broader Eurozone economy, is also sensitive to the performance of Germany's export-oriented manufacturing sector. A strengthening euro can sometimes hinder German exports by making them more expensive.

Numerical Case Study: A depreciation in the JPY can sometimes coincide with rallies in Japanese equities (Nikkei 225), as investors anticipate improved earnings prospects for Japanese exporters.

3. Safe Havens and Sentiment: Currencies as Refuges

In times of global turmoil or economic uncertainty, investors often flock to perceived safe-haven currencies, causing them to appreciate.

Swiss Franc (CHF): Famed for its neutrality and stable financial system, the Swiss franc is a classic safe-haven currency. During periods of heightened risk aversion, the CHF tends to strengthen against riskier currencies.

Japanese Yen (JPY): Despite its export sensitivity, the yen can sometimes behave as a safe haven due to Japan's large holdings of foreign assets. Market stress can trigger repatriation of funds by Japanese investors, boosting the yen.

4. The Weight of Interest Rates: Currencies and Yields

Interest rate differentials between countries play a pivotal role in FX markets. Currencies of nations with higher interest rates tend to attract capital inflows, driving up their exchange rates.

United States (USD): When the Federal Reserve raises interest rates, the US dollar often becomes more attractive compared to currencies with lower yields. This dynamic can lead to USD appreciation.

Numerical Case Study: In 2023, the aggressive interest rate hikes in the US contributed to a significant rally in the US Dollar Index (DXY) against other major currencies.

Caveats and Complexities

It's crucial to recognize that sector-specific analysis is just one piece of the FX puzzle. These points are worth noting:

Interlinkages: Sectors are rarely silos; they are interconnected within a broader economy. A slowdown in manufacturing, for instance, can impact demand for commodities.
Central Bank Policy: Interest rate decisions and monetary interventions by central banks massively influence FX markets.
Geopolitics: Wars, trade disputes, and political upheaval introduce volatility and can override sectoral trends.

Chapter 8: The Power of Sentiment Analysis

Market Sentiment Indicators: A Forex Trader's Toolkit

In the ever-volatile realm of foreign exchange (FX), success hinges on more than just technical analysis. Accurately gauging market sentiment—the prevailing mood or attitude of investors toward a particular currency pair—is a powerful weapon in a trader's arsenal. This guide delves into two key sentiment indicators: the Commitment of Traders (COT) Report and theVIX Index.

The Commitment of Traders Report: Unmasking Institutional Bias

The COT Report, issued weekly by the Commodity Futures Trading Commission (CFTC), offers a rare glimpse into the positioning of major players in the futures market. It breaks down traders into three categories:

Commercials: Large corporations and hedgers using futures to manage currency risk.
Non-Commercials: Large speculators, often hedge funds.
Non-Reportables: Small speculators.
Decoding the COT

Analyzing the COT Report for FX insights centers on the net positioning (long positions minus short positions) of non-commercials. Here's why:

Contrarian Tool: Non-commercials are often viewed as trend followers. Extreme net-long or net-short positioning can signal potential market reversals.

Directional Clues: Shifts in positioning can hint at market sentiment changes. For example, if non-commercials were heavily net-long EUR/USD, a sudden shift towards net-short might suggest waning bullish sentiment.

Case Study: GBP/USD Reversal

Let's imagine the COT Report shows non-commercials holding an extremely net-long position on GBP/USD. Historically, such extremes have often preceded bearish reversals in the pair. This information, combined with technical analysis, could strengthen a trader's conviction to enter a short position.

Source: CFTC Website (https://www.cftc.gov/)

The VIX Index: Fear Factor

Often dubbed the "fear gauge," the VIX Index measures implied volatility in the S&P 500 options market. Why is this relevant to FX?

Risk Sentiment Proxy: High VIX readings imply heightened fear/uncertainty among investors, which often leads to a flight to safe-haven currencies like the Japanese yen (JPY) or the Swiss franc (CHF). Conversely, low VIX readings might signal risk-on sentiment favoring higher-yielding currencies.

Correlation Clues: Studying the historical correlation between the VIX and specific currency pairs can offer valuable insights. For example, EUR/USD often exhibits a negative correlation with the VIX.

Case Study: JPY Surge Amid Market Turmoil

Suppose geopolitical tensions flare and global stock markets tank, sending the VIX soaring. Historical patterns suggest this could trigger a surge in JPY due to its safe-haven appeal, potentially leading to a sharp decline in pairs like USD/JPY.

Source: CBOE Website (https://www.cboe.com/)

Important Considerations

    One Piece of the Puzzle: Sentiment indicators should never be used in isolation. Always combine them with technical analysis, fundamental factors, and your overall market understanding.
    Delayed Reaction: The COT Report is released with a lag, reflecting positioning from the previous Tuesday. Be mindful of its limitations.
    Context is King: A spike in the VIX doesn't always translate to an immediate currency market reaction. Consider the broader macro environment.

Call to Action

Start incorporating these sentiment tools into your FX trading. Remember, the ability to read the crowd's emotions can provide a significant edge when navigating the dynamic world of currencies.

Understanding the Contrarian Approach

At its core, contrarian trading involves intentionally swimming against the current of predominant market sentiment. Contrarians believe that markets often overreact to news and events, creating temporary price dislocations ripe for profit through reversals to the mean.

Crowd Psychology: Contrarian trading strategies capitalize on the tendency of investor behavior to follow the herd. Fear and greed can result in traders piling into or out of currency pairs, driving prices far beyond their rational values.

Identifying Mispricing: The challenge for contrarians is pinpointing those moments when the market has temporarily mispriced an asset, whether it's a currency pair or another financial instrument. This requires deep market knowledge and an eye for unusual price behavior.

Strategies in Practice

Let's look at a few ways contrarian principles come into play within the foreign exchange realm.

Fade the Trend: This short-term strategy involves placing trades against a prevailing trend. A contrarian trader might sell into an unusually sharp rally or buy during a strong downtrend, expecting a pullback.

Reversal Play: Spotting a true top or bottom is the holy grail for contrarians. This is often informed by in-depth study of technical analysis and sentiment indicators to identify points of extreme optimism or pessimism.

News-Based Contrarianism: News events can trigger outsized market reactions. A savvy contrarian might look to fade what they see as an overshoot, assuming the market will eventually correct itself.

Unusual Angles and Details

To avoid sounding like run-of-the-mill chatbot content, let's spice things up:

The "Whisper Effect": Not all market sentiment is loud and obvious. Sometimes, a contrarian needs to read between the lines. Price action itself can hint at underlying skepticism or fear, even when news headlines seem overwhelmingly bullish or bearish.

Contrarianism Isn't Just Buying Low and Selling High: A contrarian might sell a currency pair they believe is still fundamentally undervalued if the rest of the market is exceptionally euphoric about it. They're not just looking for cheap prices, but places where the market consensus is likely wrong.

Personality Factor: Successful contrarians are masters of emotional discipline. The ability to buy when everyone else is panicking or sell when everyone's celebrating takes a specific character trait not everyone possesses.

Numerical Case Study

Let's imagine a scenario where the euro (EUR) spikes sharply against the US dollar (USD) in response to unexpectedly strong European economic data. Contrarian analysis might look like this:

Historical Context: Examine how EUR/USD has reacted to similar data releases in the past. Does the current move represent a multi-standard deviation event, hinting at a potential overshoot?

Sentiment Gauging: Are market commentators and traders universally bullish on the euro's prospects? Are news headlines overly exuberant?

Technical Clues: Search for technical indicators suggesting overbought conditions or even bearish divergence on price charts.

If the evidence stacks up, a contrarian might initiate a short-term short position on EUR/USD, expecting the euro to weaken as the initial hype fades.

Advanced AI & Research

Here's how to push this further:

Social Sentiment Mining: Utilize AI tools to scan social media posts and news articles for signs of overconfidence or irrational exuberance about specific currency pairs.

High Frequency Data Analysis Examine tick-by-tick market data for early signs of reversals in order flow or waning momentum.

Machine Learning for Contrarian Signal Generation: Seek out research papers or studies on machine-learning models designed to identify potential contrarian opportunities in real time.

Where to Go for More

Academic Literature: Search for papers like "Evidence on the Contrarian Trading in Foreign Exchange Markets" [https://ideas.repec.org/a/eee/ecmode/v26y2009i6p142 0-1431.html] for deeper investigations.

Contrarian Blogs/Websites: Look for niche bloggers or specialized websites that offer unusual takes on contrarian forex strategies.

Important Disclaimer
Contrarian trading is inherently risky. It requires strong market intuition and a stomach for volatility. It's essential to manage positions carefully with stop-losses.

Section III: Forex Trading Strategies

Chapter 9: Day Trading: Capturing Short-Term Moves

Riding the Waves of News

Day trading, the act of opening and closing positions within a single trading day, can be a thrilling (and potentially lucrative) endeavor in the volatile world of foreign exchange. One particularly compelling strategy is news trading, where traders attempt to capitalize on the rapid market fluctuations triggered by economic news releases or geopolitical events.

Why News Matters in Forex

The foreign exchange market is a vast tapestry woven from the economic and political threads of nations. News events have the power to jolt these threads, sending ripples of change through currency values. Here's the breakdown of why news can be so influential:

Shifting Expectations: Traders and large institutions operate based on expectations about a country's economic health. If a news release reveals data that drastically outperforms or underperforms those expectations, currency values can react swiftly.

Interest Rate Speculation: Central banks hold immense sway over currency values through interest rate decisions. News hinting at upcoming rate changes can cause traders to reposition themselves, leading to market movements.

The Element of Surprise: Unexpected events, be they political upheavals or natural disasters, can inject volatility by altering risk perceptions.

How to Trade Forex News

News trading isn't about predicting the news itself; it's about anticipating the market's reaction. Here's a simplified approach:

The Economic Calendar: Your Compass: Economic calendars (https://www.forexfactory.com/calendar) list high-impact news releases, their scheduled times, and the analyst consensus on expected figures. Focus on the events with the potential to cause the greatest deviation from expectations.

Understand the Data: Don't just memorize numbers. Research the economic indicators themselves – what they mean, how they're calculated, and what they tell us about a nation's economy. Think of this data as the fuel that could ignite market movement.

Straddling the Release: This technique involves placing both buy and sell orders ahead of the news release, positioned slightly above and below the current market price. If volatility surges, one of your orders might get filled, aiming for a quick profit as the market reacts.

Unusual Angles

The Sentiment Factor: News isn't just about hard data. Speeches by central bankers or influential figures can sometimes sway the market, even if the content alone isn't groundbreaking. Pay attention to the tone and underlying sentiment expressed.

Correlations Matter: Currency pairs don't exist in a vacuum. News affecting one country can have spillover effects on related currencies. For example, bad news for the Eurozone might indirectly strengthen the US dollar.

Case Study: The NFP Surprise

The US Non-Farm Payroll (NFP) report is a notoriously market-moving news event. Let's imagine the following scenario:

Prevailing Sentiment: The market expects a modest NFP increase of 150,000 jobs.

The Release: The actual figure comes in at 300,000 – double the expectation.

Potential Reaction: The US dollar could spike as traders anticipate the Federal Reserve becoming more likely to raise interest rates in response to a strong labor market. EUR/USD might plummet on this news.

Important Notes:

Speed is King: News traders need lightning-fast execution and low-latency data feeds to maximize potential gains.

Slippage Strikes: Volatility around news events increases slippage (the difference between your order price and its filled price). This can eat into profits.

It's Not a Sure Bet: Markets aren't always rational, and news reactions can be unpredictable. Risk management is absolutely critical.

Understanding the Twitchy Nature of Intraday FX

Day trading in the foreign exchange market isn't for the faint of heart. Unlike stocks that are bound to a company's fortunes, currencies dance to the tune of global economic forces, interest rates, and a whole host of unpredictable geopolitical quirks. This makes for a market that moves (sometimes violently!) within a single trading day.

Let's unpack why harnessing this intraday volatility is such a compelling (and risky!) game for day traders:

The Market Never Truly Sleeps: Forex trades around the clock, across global timezones. Unlike stocks with their neat opening and closing bells, there's always a market open somewhere fueling price fluctuations.

Liquidity Galore: The FX market is the most liquid in the world. This means traders can enter and exit positions quickly, a necessity for riding those intraday waves.

Leverage: A Double-Edged Sword: Forex brokers often offer high leverage. For example, a 50:1 leverage ratio means with just $1000, you're controlling $50,000 worth of currency. This amplifies both potential gains and losses, making intraday forex akin to tightrope walking.

Numerical Case Study: When the News Sends Currencies Reeling

Let's imagine the US Federal Reserve unexpectedly hikes interest rates. Here's how this can trigger an intraday frenzy:

The Dollar Soars: Traders flock to the suddenly more attractive US dollar (USD), leading to a spike in the

EUR/USD exchange rate (meaning it takes more Euros to buy one dollar).

Chain Reaction: This move in the EUR/USD pair can send shockwaves through other currencies, impacting pairs like USD/JPY and GBP/USD in complex ways.

A Day Trader's Window: The hours following the news announcement can be a whirlwind where savvy traders with tight risk management might catch swift rises or dips in various currency pairs.

Spotting the Volatility Sweet Spots

Not every currency pair offers juicy intraday movement, and timing is everything. Here's what traders look for:

Major Pairs: Focus on the heavily-traded ones like EUR/USD, GBP/USD, or USD/JPY. These tend to have the most intraday action.

Economic Announcements: Schedule major releases like interest rate decisions, unemployment data, etc. Calendar Example: ForexFactory: https://www.forexfactory.com/. The volatility often spikes around these times.

Technical Indicators to the Rescue: Tools like Average True Range (ATR), Bollinger Bands, and the Relative Strength Index (RSI) can offer clues about a currency pair's intraday "twitchiness".

Unusual Word Choices to Spice Things Up

Ditch the usual "volatile" - here are some substitutes to elevate your writing:

Erratic: "Intraday price swings in the USD/CAD pair were erratic after the Bank of Canada statement."

Mercurial: "The Pound Sterling displayed mercurial behavior against the Euro throughout the morning session."

Whimsical: "The usually stable Swiss Franc had a whimsical afternoon, reacting strongly to shifts in the Eurozone."

Chapter 10: Swing Trading: Riding the Trends

Swing Trading in FX

In the ever-shifting tides of the foreign exchange market, swing trading offers a way to navigate the medium-term trends. Identifying swing highs and lows is an essential skill for swing traders, akin to a surfer spotting the perfect wave formation.

What are Swing Highs and Lows?

Swing High: A peak in price action where the high is flanked by lower highs on both sides. It signals a temporary zenith in an uptrend.
Swing Low: A trough in price action where the low is surrounded by higher lows on both sides. It suggests a temporary floor in a downtrend.

Think of these as the pivot points where the market's momentum might shift, either continuing the trend or signaling a potential reversal.

Why Do They Matter?

Swing highs and lows provide valuable insights for forex traders:

Trend Identification: A series of higher swing highs and lows confirms an uptrend, while lower swing highs and lows confirm a downtrend.
Support and Resistance: Swing highs/lows often act as price levels where the market either bounces off (support) or struggles to break through (resistance). Spotting these levels can be crucial for entry and exit timing.

Chart Pattern Clues: Swing points can help identify chart patterns like head-and-shoulders or double tops/bottoms, which can offer further clues about trend continuation or reversals.

How to Spot Swing Highs & Lows: Techniques and Unusual Angles

Naked Eye: The most basic method is visually identifying the peaks and troughs on your charts. This works well for clear trends, but can be subjective.

Zig Zag Indicator: Many charting platforms have this built-in tool. It automatically plots swing highs and lows, adjustable for sensitivity.

Fibonacci Retracements (An Unusual Angle): After a major move, Fibonacci retracement levels (like 38.2% or 61.8%) can sometimes be spots where a trend resumes or reverses, acting as swing points.

Pivot Points (Less Common in FX): More popular with stocks, some FX traders use pivot points calculated from prior highs, lows, and closes to identify potential turning zones.

Numerical Case Study

Let's imagine EUR/USD is in an uptrend. You spot a swing high at 1.1500. Here are some ways to capitalize:

Retracement Entry: Wait for a pullback to a support level (perhaps a Fibonacci level near the previous swing low) to potentially enter a long position.

Resistance Breakout: If price blasts through 1.1500, it could signal trend continuation, potentially warranting a long position.

Trend Reversal: If price drops below the previous swing low decisively, it might indicate the uptrend is broken, suggesting a short position.

Additional Things to Keep In Mind

Timeframe Matters: Swing highs/lows are best identified on daily or 4-hour charts for swing trades lasting days to weeks.

Economic Context: Fundamental news and economic data releases can supercharge a trend or whipsaw the market, affecting swing points.

Don't Rely Solely on Swings: Use other technical indicators (e.g., RSI, MACD) to increase your confidence in any setups.

Sources for Further Study

[Babypips - Swing Highs and Lows]
Identifying Swing Highs and Lows

Remember: Swing trading is a skill honed through practice and experience. Learning to identify swing highs and lows effectively and integrating them into your FX strategies can help you ride the trends and potentially improve your outcomes.

Trend Following in FX Swing Trading

Swing trading, nestled between the frenzy of day trading and the long haul of position trading, is a practical approach for many FX traders. One particularly effective strategy within swing trading is trend following. It's less about flashy technical indicators or gut-wrenching predictions, and more about identifying and riding the prevailing waves of the notoriously volatile FX market.

The Trend is Your (Somewhat Fickle) Friend

The core principle of trend following is deceptively simple:

Uptrend: Buy assets that are on the rise.
Downtrend: Sell assets that are declining in value.

The tricky part? Trends, especially in FX, can be shifty. They change directions, stall, or reverse completely. Successful trend followers don't fight the tide; they learn to navigate its choppy waters.

Tools of the Trade: Unusual Suspects

While many trend-following traders rely on common indicators, here are a few less obvious tools to consider:

Donchian Channels: These visualize price volatility by plotting upper and lower bands around recent price action. Breakouts above or below these bands can signal potential trend changes. Think of them as the "riverbanks" of a price trend. [Source: Investopedia - Donchian Channels] (https://www.investopedia.com/terms/d/donchianchannels.asp)

Keltner Channels: Similar to Donchian Channels, but instead of fixed bands, they use average true range (ATR) to adjust the channel width in response to market volatility. A breakout outside the Keltner Channel might indicate a significant trend shift. Source: Investopedia - Keltner Channel: https://www.investopedia.com/terms/k/keltnerchannel.asp

Parabolic SAR: A slightly more complex indicator, but helpful for identifying potential reversals. It places dots above or below price candles, with changing dot positions hinting at trend shifts. [Source: Investopedia - Parabolic SAR] ([invalid URL removed])

Case Study: The EUR/USD Rollercoaster

Let's imagine a hypothetical scenario based on recent EUR/USD trends:

Initial signal: In early 2023, the Donchian Channel on your daily chart shows a decisive price breakout above the upper band, suggesting an emerging uptrend.

Entry: You open a long position on EUR/USD, anticipating further appreciation.

Monitoring: You use the Keltner Channel as a volatility gauge. The price remains comfortably within the channel for several weeks, confirming the trend's strength.

Potential Exit: Suddenly, the Parabolic SAR dots flip below the price candles. This, combined with a narrowing Keltner Channel, suggests the uptrend might be weakening. You consider closing your position to lock in profits.

The Art of Imperfect Timing

Trend following isn't about nailing the absolute tops and bottoms of a market move. It's about recognizing the overall direction and making informed trades to capture a significant portion of the trend. There will be false signals and unexpected reversals – that's the nature of FX.

Key Mindsets for Trend-Following Success

Patience is Profitable: Waiting for clear trend signals reduces the risk of getting whipsawed by market noise. Impulsive decisions are often punished in FX.

Discipline Over Discretion: Predefined rules for entry, exit, and risk management help you avoid emotionally driven trades. Having a system lets you navigate the inevitable emotional swings of the market.

Risk is Your Rudder: Trend following shouldn't be reckless. Strict stop-losses and calculated position sizes protect you from the sudden storms of the FX market.

Beyond the Basics

This is just a glimpse into the world of trend-following for FX swing traders. Here are a few areas for further investigation that could yield unique insights:

Multi-timeframe analysis: How do long-term trends on weekly charts inform your shorter-term swing trading decisions?

Sentiment indicators: Can tools that measure market optimism/pessimism provide early clues of potential reversals?

Correlations: How do trends in related markets (like commodities or other currencies) influence your FX trend-following strategies?

Why Bother With Multiple Timeframes?

Think of analyzing a market in a single timeframe as akin to driving with tunnel vision.

Filtering Noise: Lower timeframes (like 1-minute or 5-minute charts) are full of market 'noise' – small, erratic fluctuations that can distract from the bigger picture. Higher timeframes smooth out this noise, revealing the overarching direction.

Confirming Signals: What seems like a great trade setup on a 1-hour chart might actually contradict the prevailing trend on a daily or weekly chart. Multiple timeframes help cross-check signals and increase the probability of a successful trade.

Aligning with Your Goals: Swing traders need a balance between spotting decent-sized trends and not waiting forever for trades to play out. Multiple timeframes help tailor your analysis to suit this specific style.

The "Top-Down" Approach

One common way to use multiple timeframes is the 'top-down' approach. Here's the gist:

Start Global: Begin with a weekly or even monthly chart to grasp the dominant, long-term trend of a currency pair. Is it an uptrend, downtrend, or ranging within a sideways channel?

Zero-In: Move down to daily charts for a medium-term perspective. Identify key support and resistance levels relevant to your swing trading timeframe.

Seek Your Entry: Switch to your preferred trade execution timeframe (common ones include 4-hour or 1-hour charts). Look for buy or sell signals that align with the broader trend you identified on the higher timeframes.

Case Study (Hypothetical): EUR/USD

Let's imagine this scenario:

Weekly Chart: EUR/USD shows a clear downtrend with lower highs and lower lows.

Daily Chart: Price is approaching a major resistance zone that previously halted rallies.

4-Hour Chart: A bearish candlestick pattern forms near the daily resistance, suggesting a potential shorting opportunity.

With the multi-timeframe analysis, you'd feel more confident in a short trade, as your entry aligns with the overall downtrend.

Numerical Considerations

While not everyone agrees on fixed rules, a common guideline for swing trading timeframes is:

Higher Timeframe: Daily or Weekly
Medium Timeframe: 4-Hour or 12-Hour
Execution Timeframe: 1-Hour

Another element to consider is your risk tolerance. A smaller stop-loss (dictated by your execution timeframe analysis) combined with a wider, trend-based target (from your higher timeframe) is a hallmark of swing trading.

Unusual Angles and Word Choices

"Timeframe Tango": Trading is often about rhythm. Using multiple timeframes is like dancing with the market at different tempos.

"The Magnifying Glass Effect": Higher timeframes bring broader trends into focus, lower timeframes let you scrutinize the details.

Important Notes

No One-Size-Fits-All: The specific timeframes you choose depend on your individual trading style and preferences.
Practice Makes Perfect: Backtesting and paper trading is crucial for seeing how this all plays out in practice before you risk real money.

Sources (Remember: Always double-check these before using them)

[Investopedia on Multiple Timeframe Analysis] (https://www.investopedia.com/articles/forex/08/multiple-timeframe.asp)
[YouTube Channels on Swing Trading] (Search for reputable channels)

Setting Wider Stop Losses and Profit Targets in Swing Trading

Swing trading, in the fast-paced world of forex, is a game of calculated patience. It's about identifying those larger market trends and attempting to ride them out, unlike the rapid-fire decisions of day trading. But, within swing trading, there's an art to balancing risk and reward, and that's where stop losses and profit targets take center stage.

The Vocabulary of Protection: Stop Losses

A stop loss is your safety net. It's an order that says "If the price drops to this level, get me out of this trade." In swing trading, the idea of using wider stop losses might seem counterintuitive. After all, wouldn't tighter stops limit your losses?

Here's the twist: Forex markets are notoriously volatile. Currency pairs can have sudden, sharp movements due to news, economic releases, or even just random fluctuations. A tight stop loss risks getting you kicked out of a trade prematurely, just because of a temporary blip on the chart.

Wider stop losses are like giving your trade some breathing room.

Numerical Case Study

Let's say you're bullish on the EUR/USD pair. You enter a long position at 1.0500. Here's how stop-loss placement changes things:

Tight stop loss: Placed at 1.0450 (50 pips below entry)

Wider stop loss: Placed at 1.0350 (150 pips below entry)

If the market suddenly drops to 1.0455, the tight stop loss triggers, closing your trade with a small loss. But, let's say that drop was just a shakeout before the EUR/USD resumes its upward climb. With the wider stop loss, your trade survives the hiccup and continues riding the trend.

Profit Targets: Locking in Those Gains

On the flip side, profit targets are like saying, "I've made enough, time to close out and enjoy the fruits of my labor." Unlike stop losses, which are primarily about protection, profit targets are where greed and discipline collide.

With swing trading, since you're aiming for larger moves, wider profit targets make sense. You're not trying to snatch a few pips; you want to capture a substantial chunk of the trend.

The Psychology of "Letting Your Winners Run"

There's an adage in trading: "Cut your losses short and let your winners run." Wider stop losses help with the first part, but wider profit targets are essential for the latter. It takes mental fortitude to watch a trade climb higher and higher without prematurely snatching a small profit for fear of the market reversing.

Sources to Consider

Babypips - Swing Trading:
https://www.babypips.com/forexpedia/swing-trading
Investopedia - Swing Trading:
https://www.investopedia.com/how-to-swing-trade-7378179

Advanced Considerations

Trailing Stop Losses: Instead of fixed stop-loss points, consider trailing stops. These adjust dynamically as the market moves in your favor, locking in some profit while still allowing for further gains.

Technical Analysis: Wider stops and targets need to be informed by technical analysis of charts. Look for key support/resistance zones, trendlines, etc., to make placement decisions.

Volatility Filters: Some currency pairs are more volatile than others. Wider stops losses might be especially important for those pairs.

Remember: There's no one-size-fits-all answer for stop loss and profit target placement. It's a balancing act informed by market conditions, your chosen pair, and your own risk tolerance.

Risk Management for Swing Trading in Foreign Exchange

Swing trading, with its focus on riding medium-term trends in the forex market, can be a thrilling way to navigate the often-volatile waters of currency exchange. However, any seasoned trader knows that success hinges on masterful risk management. Without careful strategies, those promising trends can turn into treacherous riptides, dragging your profits down into the depths.

Let's explore some key concepts and unconventional approaches to help you outsmart the risks inherent in forex swing trading.

Key Concepts: Not Your Grandma's Risk Management

Embrace the Volatility Monster: Forex markets aren't known for their cuddly personalities. Swings can be amplified compared to other markets. Understanding and planning for this volatility is essential, rather than fearing it.

The "Overnight Gap" Gremlin: Unlike some markets, forex trades 24/5. That means a position held overnight could open with an unpleasant "gap" (sudden price jump) against you the next day, especially around weekends.

Position Sizing is Your Best Friend: Don't gamble your whole account on a single trade, no matter how tempting. Smaller, calculated position sizes will weather temporary drawdowns better.

Numerical Case Study: When Things Go South

Imagine you're bullish on EUR/USD. You buy 100,000 EUR hoping for a rise against the dollar. Let's consider a few scenarios:

Scenario 1: Minor Dip Price drops by 50 pips (that's forex lingo for tiny price moves). With proper position sizing, let's say a 1% maximum risk per trade, your loss is around $50. Manageable.

Scenario 2: The Gap A weekend news event tanks EUR/USD by 200 pips. With the same risk strategy, that's a $200 loss. Stinging, but survivable.

Scenario 3: All Bets Off You threw caution to the wind, risking 10% on this trade. That 200 pip gap translates to a $2000 hit. Ouch! This could wipe out a small account.

Tools and Techniques: Your Risk-Taming Arsenal

Stop-Loss Orders: Your Digital Bodyguard These orders automatically close your trade if the price moves against you by a preset amount. Non-negotiable for swing trading!

Trailing Stops: The Profit-Protector This type of stop-loss adjusts upwards as your trade moves in your favor, locking in gains while still allowing for some breathing room.

Leverage: Use with Extreme Caution: Leverage multiplies both potential gains AND losses. Swing traders should consider moderate leverage (if at all) to avoid wild swings in their account balance.

Diversification: Don't Bet the Farm on One Currency Pair Spreading your trades across slightly uncorrelated pairs can help soften the blow if one trade goes sideways. Unexpected Angles: Beyond the Basics

Correlations Matter: Keep tabs on how your chosen currency pair interacts with others, and major assets like gold or oil. Surprises in related markets could impact your trade.

News Isn't Always the Boogeyman: While sudden news can cause gaps, scheduled releases (interest rates, economic data) can sometimes be anticipated, allowing for adjusted risk strategies.

The Psychology Factor Swing trading timelines can mess with your emotions. Greed and fear can lead to abandoning your risk plan. Develop mental strategies alongside technical ones.

Sources (Remember to Verify!)

https://www.babypips.com/learn/forex/swing-trading
Investopedia: Understanding Forex Leverage: https://www.investopedia.com/ask/answers/06/forexle verage.asp
FXCM: Economic Calendar: https://www.fxcm.com/markets/research/economic-calendar/

Let's Get Weird: Unusual Tips

Embrace "Demo" Trading: It's like the training wheels for risk management. Practice with fake money to build your risk instincts before risking real capital.

Chart the Weirder Timeframes: Most traders focus on daily charts. Look at weekly or even monthly charts to spot larger trends potentially hidden in the daily noise.

Set a "Stupidity Tax": Force yourself to pay a small penalty (real or to charity) every time you violate your risk plan. Pain is a great teacher!

Chapter 11: Position Trading: The Long-Term View

Carry Trade Strategies

In the realm of foreign exchange (FX), the carry trade is a time-tested strategy with a deceptively simple principle: you borrow a currency with a low interest rate. The goal is to pocket the difference, often amplified by leverage for greater returns (and heightened risk).

Position trading takes a longer view than the rapid-fire pace of day trading or scalping. Carry trades within a position trading approach have unique considerations. Let's delve into the nuances, potential pitfalls, and unusual tactics that can refine your FX carry trade strategy for a longer investment horizon.

The Nature of the Carry Trade Beast

Volatility's Double-Edged Sword: Carry trades can be lucrative in low-volatility periods, but wilder market swings can quickly turn profits into losses. A long-term approach necessitates careful analysis of a currency pair's volatility profile and understanding when carry trade benefits might be negated.

The Trend is Your... (Sometimes) Friend: Carry trades can work with or against prevailing trends. Riding a trend can yield additional pip gains from the currency appreciation, but sharp trend reversals can be devastating.

The Specter of "Unwinding": Large-scale unwinding of carry trades, often triggered by major economic events, can cause sudden, dramatic shifts in the FX market. Position traders need to be aware of this risk and its potential impact on open carry positions.

Metrics and Data-Driven Decisions

Carry trades in position trading demand a deeper level of analysis than simpler strategies. Here's where quantitative data becomes crucial:

Interest Rate Differentials: Scrutinize forward interest rate differentials, not just current spot rates. These reflect market expectations of future interest rates and are better indicators of long-term profitability.
    Source: Central bank websites, sites like Bloomberg (https://www.bloomberg.com/)
Historical Volatility: Examine a currency pair's historical volatility to gauge potential risk. Don't just rely on averages; look for periods of extreme volatility and how the pair behaved during those times.
    Source: Trading platforms (charts often include volatility indicators), dedicated volatility calculators
Fundamental Analysis: Don't overlook the economic fundamentals of the countries behind the currencies. Strong economic indicators can signal potential long-term appreciation that complements your carry trade gains.
    Data Sources: Country-specific economic data providers, financial news outlets

Case Study: The AUD/JPY Carry Trade (Numbers Tell a Story)

Let's assume you initiated an AUD/JPY carry trade position in early 2023, borrowing Japanese yen at a near-zero interest rate and investing in Australian dollars, then with a yield around 3.25%.

Scenario 1: Smooth Sailing - If the AUD/JPY exchange rate remains relatively stable, your carry trade would generate a consistent profit from the interest rate difference.

Scenario 2: Volatility Strikes - A sharp spike in the pair's volatility, perhaps triggered by an unexpected interest rate hike in Japan, could eat into your gains from the interest differential.

Scenario 3: Appreciation Bonus - If the AUD appreciates against the JPY over your position's lifespan, the extra profit on exchange rate movement is amplified alongside your carry trade returns.

Unusual Angles and Advanced Tactics

Cross-Currency Carry: Explore less conventional carry trades involving three currencies. For instance, borrowing JPY, converting to USD, then investing in higher-yielding emerging market currencies

Hedging: Partially hedging your carry trade position with options or futures contracts can mitigate volatility risk, though this naturally decreases potential profit.

Technical Indicators: While not a sole basis for decisions, technical indicators like moving averages and trendlines can provide insight into potential points for entering or exiting a long-term carry trade.

Important Reminders

Leverage Magnifies Everything: Use leverage judiciously in position trading. While it amplifies gains, it dramatically increases losses too.

Nothing is Evergreen: Interest rate differentials change, economies evolve. Continuously reassess your open positions and the suitability of carry trades in the prevailing market conditions.

Macroeconomic Trend Analysis

Position trading, unlike its scalping and day trading cousins, involves holding trades for extended periods, sometimes weeks or months. This requires a different mindset, one less focused on fleeting market noise and more attuned to those tectonic shifts in the global economy that can shape exchange rates over time.

Let's explore some key concepts and potential angles when dissecting macroeconomic factors for long-term FX opportunities.

1. The "Twin Ds": Deficits and Debt

Fiscal Deficits and FX: Large, sustained government budget deficits often mean a currency must constantly be issued (printed) to cover the shortfall. This can dilute its international value, leading to potential depreciation – an area worth scrutinizing when looking for weakness in currencies.

Unusual Angle: Instead of focusing on the headline deficit, look at structural deficits – the persistent gap between spending and income even in good economic times. This offers insight into long-term government solvency.

National Debt: A towering mountain of national debt can signal trouble ahead for a currency, particularly if it creates concerns around sovereign default. Rising interest rates needed to service the debt can further hurt a currency.

Unusual Angle: Explore the composition of national debt. High foreign-currency debt means a country must generate strong FX inflows to meet its obligations – a vulnerability that markets exploit.

2. Interest Rates: More Than Meets the Eye

The Obvious: Higher interest rates attract investors seeking returns, boosting demand and potentially the value of the currency. This is the textbook principle, but it's not that simple.

The "Real" Deal: Focus not on nominal rates, but on inflation-adjusted real interest rates. A country with 10% interest rates but 15% inflation offers a negative real return, making it less attractive to investors.

Case Study (Hypothetical): If Country A offers 3% rates and has 1% inflation, while Country B offers 6% with 4% inflation, Country A would likely be the more appealing choice for long-term FX investors.

The Unseen Hand: Central bank policy is key. Look for clues about future rate changes in speeches, economic forecasts, and meeting minutes. Is a shift to rate cuts on the horizon? This could signal potential long-term currency depreciation.

3. "Safe Havens" and the Flight to Quality

Not Just the USD and JPY: Traditionally in times of stress, investors park money in the US dollar or Japanese yen. But this isn't set in stone – other currencies, like the Swiss franc, can gain safe-haven status.

What Makes a Safe Haven?: Analyze these factors:
   Political Stability and Rule of Law
   Economic Strength and Resilience
   Deep, Liquid Financial Markets

Unusual Angle: Examine smaller "safe havens" that might fly under the radar, potentially offering better returns during crises than the stalwarts. Research the currencies of well-run commodity exporters as possible candidates.

4. Terms of Trade: Hidden Flows

Exporters vs Importers: The price difference between what a country exports and what it imports greatly influences its currency flows. This is its terms of trade.

Commodity Powerhouses: A sharp rise in the prices of a country's key exports (often commodities) tends to strengthen its currency. Conversely, a reliance on expensive commodity imports can be a drag.

Case Study: Track the terms of trade for a country like Australia (largely a commodity exporter). Favorable terms would support long-term positions in the AUD, all else equal.

Unexpected Angle: Examine a country's "economic complexity". A nation exporting diverse, high-tech goods may be more resilient and have a more stable currency than a commodity-only exporter.

Important Notes:

Don't Confuse Correlation with Causation: Spotting a macroeconomic trend is one thing; understanding why it moves markets is another. Research helps.

The Future Ain't What It Used to Be: The world changes. Established relationships can break down, so challenge your assumptions.

Technical Analysis Matters, Too: Even for long-term trades, technicals offer important entry/exit signals and risk control.

Sources:

International Monetary Fund (IMF): https://www.imf.org/en/Home
World Bank Economic Data: http://data.worldbank.org
Trading Economics: https://tradingeconomics.com/

Fundamental Analysis for Position Trading

Most folks in Forex get dazzled by technical analysis—those fancy charts and squiggly lines. But if you wanna hold positions for weeks, months, maybe even years, you gotta get down and dirty with the real drivers of currency values: fundamental analysis.

Understanding the Big Picture

Fundamental analysis is like figuring out a country's economic health checkup. You're not just looking at a snapshot, you're digging into the long-term trends that make a currency tick. Think of it like this:

Economic Growth: A booming economy (rising GDP) usually signals a strong currency. Why? Investors love growth, and a healthy economy attracts those sweet, sweet investment dollars.

Interest Rates: Imagine interest rates as the "rent" charged on money. Higher interest rates tend to make a currency more attractive, since investors can park their cash and get a better return.

Inflation: The silent wealth-sapper. High inflation erodes the buying power of a currency, making it less desirable. Like the stock market hates uncertainty, currencies hate runaway inflation.

Political Stability: Investors get skittish in shaky political climates. Stable governments with strong institutions tend to inspire confidence, boosting their currency.

Beyond the Textbook: Unusual Angles

The classics are important, but to stand out, you gotta dig deeper:

"Weathering the Storm" Factor: Some currencies, call 'em "safe havens" (like the Swiss Franc or Japanese Yen), tend to strengthen during global turmoil. Why? Investors run for cover.

Commodity Connection: If a country's economy relies heavily on exporting stuff like oil or copper, its currency will dance to the tune of those commodity prices.

Debt Worries: Too much debt? That's a red flag for investors. A heavily indebted country might have trouble repaying, weakening its currency in the long run.

Case Study: The Surprising Rise of the [Insert Less-Common Currency]

Let's say you noticed [insert a less-discussed currency, maybe Brazilian Real or South African Rand?] has been quietly gaining against the majors, despite some economic headwinds. Here's where your fundamental sleuthing skills kick in:

Dig into Interest Rates: Turns out, [country's] central bank hiked rates way more aggressively than expected to combat inflation. This makes their currency a tempting place to park cash.

Commodity Boom: A surprise surge in [key commodity that country exports] has boosted its trade balance, giving its currency an unexpected edge.

Improving Sentiment: Maybe a recent political development signals greater stability than previously thought. Investors are subtly starting to change their perception.

Key Takeaway: It's not just about the numbers – it's about connecting the dots, finding those under-the-radar changes that the market's not fully priced in yet.

Words of Caution

Beware the "Hype Train": News headlines love to scream about the latest crisis or economic miracle. Don't get suckered into knee-jerk reactions. Position trading is about the slow burn, not the flash fire.

No Such Thing as a Sure Bet: Even with the best analysis, things can go sideways. That's the nature of Forex. It's about calculated risks, not guarantees.

Sources

Investopedia - Fundamental Analysis: https://www.investopedia.com/fundamental-analysis-4689757

International Monetary Fund (IMF) for global economic data: https://www.imf.org/en/Home

Trading Economics for interest rates and inflation figures: https://tradingeconomics.com/

[Specialized news sites for commodities, if relevant to your case study]

Holding Trades in Position Trading

Unlike hyperactive day trading or swing trading, position trading in the forex market takes a "set it and mostly forget it" approach. Position traders seek to ride major currency trends over weeks, months, or even years. It's akin to betting on a marathon runner's overall win, rather than the speed of every stride.

Why the Long Game?

Taming Volatility: Forex is notoriously choppy. Short-term fluctuations can whipsaw traders. Position trading smooths out the bumps like shock absorbers on a dirt road.

Harnessing Fundamentals: Economic forces like interest rates, inflation, and political climates drive currency value over the long haul. Position traders try to align with those fundamental tides.

Less Time = More Life: Constant monitoring is exhausting. This style suits folks with busy schedules who still want market exposure.

Unusual Nuances of Forex Position Trading

The Carry Trade Angle: A classic position trading strategy is the "carry trade". This involves borrowing in a currency with rock-bottom interest rates and buying a higher-yielding currency. You essentially pocket the interest rate difference. Of course, currency moves can negate the profit or cause losses!

The Ever-Moving Target: Unlike stocks, where a company's success can skyrocket its value, forex is more of a continuous tug-of-war. There are limited scenarios where one currency utterly collapses against another over a sustained period. Expectations in position trading need to be tempered.

Swap-Savvy: Holding positions overnight incurs "swap fees" (positive or negative) depending on interest rate differentials between currency pairs. This can eat into returns or provide a surprising bonus over time.

Case Studies (Hypothetical – Verify Current Rates)

Scenario 1: Interest Rate Play Let's say the US Federal Reserve hikes rates to 6%, while Japan's central bank keeps rates near zero. A position trader might borrow Japanese yen (JPY) cheaply and buy US dollars (USD), hoping to profit from the 6% interest and possible USD strengthening vs. JPY.

Scenario 2: Geopolitical Hedge Imagine rising tensions between the US and China. A position trader, fearing a weakening USD, could convert some USD holdings to stable Swiss Francs (CHF), betting on relative safety.

Scenario 3: Commodity Connection A trader bullish on oil prices might simultaneously establish a long position in the Canadian Dollar (CAD), as Canada is a major oil exporter. Oil price gains could amplify CAD appreciation.

Words to Spice Things Up

Rather than "profit/loss," try "harvest gains" or "weather a drawdown." Instead of "forex pair," occasionally use "currency cross." Consider a phrase like "swimming with the fundamental current" instead of simply aligning trades with economic trends.

Critical Warnings

Leverage is a Double-Edged Sword: It magnifies both wins and losses in position trading. Use it judiciously.

The Unpredictable Intrudes: Black swan events (pandemics, wars) can upend the most considered long-term trade. Position trading is NOT risk-free.

Patience is Paramount: It can be psychologically challenging to sit through sizable drawdowns even if your fundamental thesis is still sound.

Sources (Remember to Verify Before Finalizing)

Investopedia - Carry Trade: https://www.investopedia.com/carry-trade-definition-4682656
Babypips - Forex Swap Rates Explained: https://www.babypips.com/forexpedia/rollover

Next Steps: Your Further Investigation

Deep-dive into a specific currency cross for fundamental analysis (e.g., macroeconomics of EUR/USD)
Backtesting position trading rules using historical forex data
Explore risk-management techniques that fit a long-term style

Long-term Portfolio Management in Forex

Most people think of Forex trading as lightning-fast transactions – traders glued to computer screens, capitalizing on tiny price shifts. But there's another way: position trading. It's like comparing a nimble speedboat to a sturdy ocean liner. Position traders hold onto their trades for weeks, months, or even years. This strategy suits those who want to make Forex a part of a larger, well-diversified investment portfolio.

Why Position Trading?

Less Stress: Shorter timeframes demand laser-sharp focus and can mean emotionally draining roller coasters. Position trading offers a calmer experience.

Fits Other Commitments: It's perfect for people with busy jobs or lifestyles. No need to stare at charts all day; check in periodically, that's enough.

Big-Picture Focus: Position trades ride out short-term noise, aiming for major market trends fueled by fundamentals.

Building a Position Trading Portfolio

The idea is akin to stock portfolio management, but applied to currencies. Here's how:

Diversify Across Pairs: Don't put your eggs in one basket. Spread investments across different currency pairs. Consider these:

Majors: Highly liquid, good for beginners (EUR/USD, USD/JPY, GBP/USD)

Commodity-Pairs: Linked to resources (AUD/USD, NZD/USD - affected by commodity prices)

Exotics: Less common, good for experienced traders looking for extra risk/reward (USD/TRY, USD/MXN)

Correlation is Key: "Correlation" means how closely prices of different pairs move together. You want some negative correlation to spread risk. A portfolio where everything moves in lockstep is vulnerable.
Example: AUD/USD (Australian Dollar) might have a negative correlation with USD/CHF (Swiss Franc) over time as their economies respond differently to global events.

Risk Per Trade: It's never about picking winners all the time. Manage the potential damage on the trades that don't work out. Strict stop-loss orders limit your downside.
Case Study: A 2% risk rule means on a $10,000 account, no trade should lose more than $200 at its worst point.

Technical vs. Fundamental Analysis

Position traders use both chart patterns and economic data:

Technicals: Charts reveal historical price trends. These aren't foolproof, but they offer clues to likely support/resistance areas where prices may turn.
Tools: Moving averages, trendlines, candlestick patterns
Fundamentals: Economic news releases are the big drivers for long-term currency values. Keep an eye on:
Interest Rates: Higher rates generally strengthen a currency.
GDP Growth: A healthy economy boosts its currency.

Trade Balances: A country exporting more than it imports signals a strong currency.

Case Study: AUD/USD and the Iron Ore Connection

Australia is a major iron ore exporter, much of it going to China. Here's a position trading idea:

Fundamental Signal: Chinese economic data hints at increased construction activity -> demand for iron ore rises

Technical Setup: AUD/USD chart breaks above a key resistance line, hinting at an uptrend.

The Trade: Buy AUD/USD, target profit based on longer-term chart patterns, stop-loss placed to manage risk

The Mind of a Position Trader

Patience is the name of the game. Big moves take time. This also means:

Handling Drawdowns: Even good strategies have losing periods. This is normal; don't panic-sell.

Compounding Over Time: Position trading isn't about getting rich quick. Aim for slow, steady profits that snowball as you reinvest.

Position Sizing is Powerful: Increasing how much you invest per trade amplifies profits (but also risk). Start with smaller sizes until your track record warrants going larger.

Additional Notes:

Reliable Broker: Choose one with good spreads (the difference between buying/selling price) and low fees.

Swap Rates: These are overnight interest fees when you hold trades for extended periods. Factor them into your profit/loss calculations

Sources for Further Research

[https://www.babypips.com/]
Investopedia on Position Trading

Chapter 12: Building a Personalized Trading Plan

Understanding Risk Tolerance

Risk tolerance is an absolutely critical – yet often misunderstood – concept in the world of forex trading. It's about how much financial volatility you're comfortable enduring to potentially achieve your trading goals. It's NOT about being a risk-taker or a thrill-seeker. Understanding your risk tolerance is the first step towards building a trading plan that genuinely aligns with who you are as an investor.

Key Factors Influencing Your Risk Tolerance

Financial Situation: Your income, savings, debt level, and overall financial stability all play a role in how much risk you can realistically take on.

Investment Goals: Are you aiming for short-term gains or long-term wealth building? Higher-risk strategies might be appropriate for quick profits, but a greater emphasis on stability is usually better for long-term goals.

Personality: Are you naturally cautious or more inclined to take calculated risks? Your emotional makeup matters in the volatile world of forex markets.

Market Knowledge: The more you understand forex, the better equipped you are to make informed risk assessments.

Assessing Your Risk Tolerance

There's no single "right" way to assess your risk tolerance. Here are a few approaches:

Risk Tolerance Questionnaires: Many online brokerages offer questionnaires. These can help you start thinking critically about your comfort level with risk.

Hypothetical Scenarios: Think through questions like: "If my initial investment drops by 20% in a month, how would I feel?"

Historical Analysis: Look at your past financial decisions. Have you tended towards stability-focused investments, or are you a seasoned risk-taker?

Case Study: The Contrasting Cases of Sarah and Alex

Sarah: Sarah is a single mother with significant student loan debt. She wants to grow her savings, but also needs financial security. Her forex plan should focus on conservative strategies, minimizing drawdowns (temporary losses).

Alex: Alex is a young professional with high disposable income and few financial obligations. He's looking for aggressive growth. He may be comfortable with riskier strategies, but needs to implement strict stop-losses to manage that risk responsibly.

Integrating Risk Tolerance in Your Trading Plan

Your risk tolerance should shape every aspect of your forex plan:

Position Sizing: How much will you risk on a single trade? Conservative traders might risk 1-2% of their account balance per trade, while more aggressive traders might go higher.

Leverage: Leverage magnifies both potential gains and losses. Low-risk traders should keep leverage minimal.

Currency Pair Selection: Major currency pairs (like EUR/USD) tend to be less volatile than exotic pairs or those involving emerging market currencies.

Trade Duration: Scalping (very short-term trades) is inherently riskier than swing trading or position trading.

Ways to Make Your Writing Stand Out

Unexpected Analogies: Compare risk management to seat belts – both protect you from catastrophic outcomes.

Embrace the Counterintuitive: Discuss how a high risk tolerance trader might actually be MORE disciplined than someone less comfortable with volatility.

"Oddball" Vocabulary: Consider words like "sangfroid" (composure under pressure) to break from generic financial jargon.

Important Notes:

Risk tolerance is dynamic: It can change with your life circumstances. Review your plan regularly.

There's no substitute for education: The better you understand forex, the more informed your risk decisions will be.

Sources

Investopedia on Risk Tolerance: https://www.investopedia.com/articles/pf/07/risk_toler ance.asp

Examples of Risk Tolerance Questionnaires: https://assets.tastyworks.com/production/documents/d ay_trading_risk_disclosure.pdf

Determining Financial Goals

The foreign exchange (forex) market thrums with possibility, but harnessing that potential demands a crystal-clear understanding of your financial aims. A tailored trading plan without well-defined goals is like a ship without a compass – drifting, not navigating.

Let's explore how to set achievable, motivating financial goals that align with your unique forex journey.

Thinking Beyond Dollar Signs

While dollar figures immediately come to mind, don't let those be your sole focus. Consider these less-obvious goals:

   Preservation of Capital: Especially for beginners, a primary goal might be to avoid significant losses during the learning phase. Success might look like maintaining 90% of your starting capital over the first six months.
   Consistency Trumps Windfalls: One wildly profitable trade doesn't build a career. Aim for steady, smaller gains. A target like "average 2% positive return per month" can be far more achievable than chasing moonshots.
   Skill Mastery: Learning forex takes time. Set goals around mastering concepts like technical analysis, market sentiment, or risk management. These skills are your long-term meal ticket.

Numerical Case Studies

Let's illustrate the power of goal-setting with a few scenarios:

Scenario 1: The Preservationist

   Starting Capital: $5,000
   Primary Goal: Maintain 95% of capital over 12 months while learning.
   Risk Tolerance: Very low (Maximum 1% of capital risked per trade)
   Success Metric: Ending the year with a minimum of $4,750, even if overall profit is minimal.

Scenario 2: The Steady Builder

   Starting Capital: $10,000
   Primary Goal: Compound monthly returns averaging 3%
   Risk Tolerance: Moderate (2-3% capital risked per trade)
   Success Metric: At year's end, account balance exceeds $14,250

Scenario 3: The Knowledge Seeker

   Starting Capital: $2,000 (primarily for educational trading)
   Primary Goal: Demonstrate mastery of three technical indicators by profitably applying them in live trades.
   Risk Tolerance: Low (1% or less capital per trade)
   Success Metric: Document trading journal showing consistent, rule-based trade execution with those indicators.

The "SMART" Advantage

Make your goals truly actionable by using the SMART framework:

Specific: "Make more money" is vague. "Increase account balance by 10% this quarter" is specific.
Measurable: Goals need trackable metrics (percentages, dollar amounts, skill benchmarks).
Achievable: Don't aim to become a millionaire overnight. Small, attainable goals build confidence.
Relevant: Goals must align with your risk tolerance and overall trading style.
Time-Bound: Attach deadlines to avoid open-ended drifting.

A Word on Psychology

The emotional side of trading can undo the best plans. Consider these factors alongside your financial goals:

Greed vs. Fear: Don't let either derail your plan. Set exit points (both profit and loss) before entering trades.
The Gambler's Fallacy: Each trade is independent. A string of losses doesn't guarantee the next one's a winner.
Revenge Trading: Don't overtrade to "make back" losses. Stick to your proven strategy.

Sources for Further Exploration

https://www.babypips.com/trading/forex-expectations-that-lead-to-disappointment-2024-01-29
Investopedia: Forex Trading Psychology: https://www.investopedia.com/trading-psychology-4689647

Important Disclaimer: Forex trading carries significant risk. Never invest more than you can afford to lose.

Capital allocation and trade sizing in forex trading

Understanding the Foundations

Capital Allocation: The process of dividing your trading funds across different currency pairs, strategies, and even across multiple accounts. It's NOT a one-size-fits-all answer!

Trade Sizing: Determining the ideal position size (how much to buy or sell) for each trade you take. The goal is to strike a balance between potential profit and manageable risk.

Why These Concepts Matter

These two are the backbone of risk management. Done poorly, even a profitable strategy can drain your account. Done well, they:

Mitigate Risk: Minimize the impact of any single trade gone wrong.

Maximize Growth Potential: Allow you to survive losing streaks and seize opportunities when your strategy has an edge.

Psychological Edge: Protect you from the emotional rollercoaster of oversized trades.

Unusual Angles to Set Your Plan Apart

Let's ditch the generic advice and explore some less common approaches:

The Volatility Angle: Instead of a fixed percentage risk per trade, adjust it based on current market volatility. If the currency pair is going haywire, take smaller positions, and vice versa when things are calm. Check out indicators like the Average True Range (ATR) to help you gauge volatility.

The "Portfolio" Mindset: Treat your forex trading like a mini-investment portfolio. Instead of thinking "per trade," allocate percentages of your capital to different currency pairs or strategies. This introduces a natural form of diversification.

The Asymmetric Approach: Not all trades are created equal. Maybe you have a high-win-rate scalping setup alongside a less frequent but incredibly profitable trend-following system. Explore risking less capital on those high-probability trades and more on the bigger, less frequent ones.

Case Study: Scaling Up

Let's say you start with $5,000 trading capital. A common (but often dangerous) rule is to risk 1% per trade, which would be $50. Now, imagine these scenarios:

Losing Streak: If you hit 5 consecutive losses, that's $250 gone – 5% of your account. That hurts, but you're still in the game.

Big Winner: A single trade nets you $500. That's a 10% return, massively boosting your account with a single move.

Numerical Considerations: The Kelly Criterion Angle

The Kelly Criterion is a controversial yet fascinating formula:

$$f = (bp - q) / b$$

Where:
    f = Fraction of account to risk
    b = Odds of winning (expressed as a decimal)
    p = Probability of winning
    q = Probability of losing

Caveats:

The Kelly Criterion is VERY sensitive to your win rate estimates.
Most traders use "half Kelly" or even less for a safety buffer.

[Source: Investopedia Kelly Criterion: https://www.investopedia.com/terms/k/kellycriterion.asp]

Beyond the Basics

Here's where things get REALLY interesting:

Correlated Currency Pairs: If you're trading EUR/USD and GBP/USD simultaneously, they move together. You need to adjust your risk exposure accordingly to avoid doubling up on risk unknowingly.
The Psychology Factor: Are you prone to revenge trading? If so, strict trade sizing rules become your safety net.

Re-evaluate Regularly: Markets shift, and your trading edge might too. Revisit your allocation strategy at set intervals (quarterly, yearly, etc.).

Important Disclaimer
There is no "magic formula" for capital allocation and trade sizing in forex markets. These concepts demand personalization based on:
Your risk tolerance
Your strategies
Your experience level

Understanding Trading Styles

Trading styles are like choosing your weapon in a battle. Each has unique strengths and fits certain warriors better than others.

Technical Analysis: The Seer

Technical traders are the chart-readers, the pattern-finders. They believe that all the information they need is in the price movements themselves. They see the market as a swirling storm of emotions, and charts are their weather maps.
Tools: Candlesticks, trends, moving averages, support/resistance, technical indicators (RSI, MACD, etc.).
Unusual Angle: Look into contrarian indicators or volume analysis (less common than price-centric stuff). Discuss the psychology behind how patterns form.

Fundamental Analysis: The Historian
These traders are deep divers. They care about a country's economic health, political earthquakes, and interest rate whispers. They believe prices are a lagging reflection of the grand world stage.

Tools: Economic reports, interest rates, central bank statements, geopolitical news.

Unusual Angle: Explore lesser-known economic indicators (think consumer confidence or manufacturing sentiment). Discuss how seemingly non-financial news (elections, natural disasters) can ripple through FX markets.

Hybrid: The Alchemist

Hybrid traders are mix-and-matchers. They understand the power of charts and the pulse of the wider world. They might use fundamentals to choose a trade, then technicals to time their entry and exit.

Tools: A blend of both worlds.

Unusual Angle: Dive into the debate about which style is "better." Highlight successful traders who surprisingly switched styles mid-career.

Why Style Matters

Your choice isn't about being right; it's about being consistent. Here's what to consider:

Personality: Are you a numbers person or a big-picture thinker? Do you thrive on quick decisions or careful research?

Time Horizon: Technicals are often favored by day traders, while fundamentals align better with position traders (holding for weeks or months).

Market Conditions: Some styles shine in trending markets, others in choppy ones. Adaptability is key!

Numerical Case Studies (Caution: These Need Fact-Checking)

The EUR/USD Plunge Fueled by News: Maybe explore how a single tweet from a central banker sent the Euro spiraling for days. Dig into the market psychology of panic selling or overreaction.

Charting the Safe-haven: Maybe examine how the Japanese Yen strengthens during global crises, and how traders visualize this on a price chart.

The Contrarian's Win: Maybe profile trader XYZ, known for buying when everyone sells and using unusual technical indicators.

Unusual Word Choices

Instead of "trend," say the market "ebbs and flows"
Replace "volatile" with "mercurial" or "fickle"
Don't say an indicator "works," say it "whispers" or "hints"

Sources to Spark Your Research:

[TradingView Blogs] (https://www.tradingview.com/blog/) - Especially the "Ideas" section.

[Investopedia] (https://www.investopedia.com) – Excellent for definitions and clear examples.

[Central Bank Websites] - Dry, but they're the source for economic data.

[Financial News Sites] - But go beyond the headlines, look for analysis of why markets moved.

Final Note

Trading is a lifelong learning curve. Your style will likely evolve alongside your experience. Don't be afraid to experiment on demo accounts, keep a trading journal, and ruthlessly analyze what works and what doesn't for you.

Harnessing the Power of Journaling & Tracking

The volatile world of Forex trading demands a trader who is not only knowledgeable but extraordinarily self-aware. Journaling and meticulous performance tracking are the often-overlooked keys to achieving this. Think of these practices as building your personal trading laboratory – a place for observation, experimentation, and refinement.

The Quirky Anatomy of a Forex Journal

Don't let "journal" conjure images of flowery diary entries. Here's a breakdown of what to include:

Trade Fundamentals:
Currency pair, date/time of entry/exit, lot size, position (long/short), price at entry and exit.
Technical Setup:
Indicators used (with settings), timeframe, chart patterns, important price levels (support/resistance).
The "Why":
YOUR rationale behind the trade. Was it a news-based play? A momentum trade? This is where brutal honesty is key.

Emotional Thermometer:

Use single words: "Calm", "Hesitant", "Greedy", etc. This builds your emotional vocabulary around trades.

Visuals:

Screenshots of your chart setup BEFORE the trade goes live are invaluable learning tools.

Trade Reflections:

Did the trade follow your plan? Where did it deviate? Could you have exited sooner/later?

Tracking: Beyond Wins and Losses

Raw profit/loss only tells part of the story. Deeper metrics unveil hidden strengths and weaknesses:

Expectancy: Average profit/loss per trade. A high positive expectancy means your system WORKS, even if your win rate is low. ([Source for expectancy calculation]:https://www.investopedia.com/articles/tradi ng/04/092204.asp).

Risk/Reward Ratio: How much you risk per trade vs. potential gain. Aim for at least 1:2 for sustainable trading.

"Feel" Metrics: Unusual here, but potent. Track things like:

Trades taken during your "peak" mental hours vs. trades taken when tired

Impact of external news/events on your emotional state during the trade

Case Study: The "Hesitation Tax"

Let's say you notice your journal is riddled with "hesitant" next to trades with small wins, yet large losses. You may be cutting profits too early and letting losers run. This is "The Hesitation Tax" – where missed potential due to fear eats into your bottom line. Your data has revealed a psychological stumbling block!

From Journal to Adaptive Plan

The true magic is the marriage of your journal and tracking to craft a trading plan that's unique to YOU:

Emotional Triggers: Your journal reveals patterns. Maybe news trades make you overly optimistic. This mandates stricter trade rules for those setups.

Pattern Recognition: Did those meticulous chart screenshots reveal a setup that consistently works in your favor? Perfect! Your plan now focuses on finding and optimizing THAT setup.

Exit Evolving: Tracking might show you consistently exit too early. Your plan now includes testing trailing stops or scaling out of positions gradually.

Tech Tools (With a Pinch of Salt)

Dedicated Journaling: Edgewonk (https://www.edgewonk.com/) is popular, but even spreadsheets work. The key is consistency.

Don't Over-Automate: AI-powered trade analysis is tempting. Remember, the goal here is to train YOUR brain, not outsource it.

Unusual Angles to Consider

Micro-Journaling: Quick notes after big market moves, even on trades you DIDN'T take. Trains your situational awareness.

The "Whoops" Trade: Deliberately take one 'bad' trade per week, the kind gut instinct screams against. The detailed postmortem analysis can be enlightening.

Key Takeaway

This is not about a rigid, one-size-fits-all solution. It's a tool for self-discovery as a trader. The Forex market evolves, and so too must your personalized plan.

Section IV: Risk Management Essentials

Chapter 13: The Psychology of Trading: Mastering Your Emotions

Common Emotional Pitfalls in Forex Trading

The foreign exchange market (forex) is a beast unlike any other. Its sheer size, lightning-fast pace, and global reach create a trading environment where fortunes are won and lost in the blink of an eye. But technical analysis and news-watching only go so far – the most dangerous enemy for the forex trader often lurks within.

Let's dive beyond the obvious "fear and greed" narrative to explore some lesser-known emotional traps that can sabotage your forex journey.

1. The Numbness of "Small Wins"

It's counterintuitive, but a string of small, consistent wins can be more dangerous than a single, gut-wrenching loss. Why? Because those tiny gains lull you into a false sense of invincibility. Gradually take on riskier trades that don't fit your plan.

Case Study: Sarah, a cautious trader, had a 3-week streak with an average 2% profit per day. Emboldened, she doubled her usual trade size... and promptly lost a week's worth of gains in a single afternoon.

Takeaway: Don't let the dopamine rush of small wins blind you to your overall risk profile.

2. Analysis Paralysis: When Fear Masquerades as Prudence

Fear isn't always about heart-pounding panic. Sometimes it disguises itself as excessive caution. You research endlessly, build elaborate models, but never actually pull the trigger on a trade.

Case Study: Michael spent months backtesting a system. The results were excellent on paper, but he kept finding reasons to delay going live – tweaking indicators, waiting for "perfect" market conditions. His opportunity cost was enormous.

Takeaway: There's a difference between due diligence and fear-driven procrastination. Set deadlines for your analysis, and have a plan to move into action.

3. The Slippery Slope of Confirmation Bias

We all gravitate toward information that confirms our existing beliefs. In forex, this translates to cherry-picking news articles that support your current trade, or downplaying data that contradicts it. Confirmation bias is a sneaky way your brain protects its ego.

Case Study: A EUR/USD trader becomes convinced the downtrend is over. They ignore reports of rising European inflation and focus solely on positive employment figures, leading to a bad trade.

Takeaway: Actively seek out disconfirming evidence. Assign a "devil's advocate" role to a trading buddy, or force yourself to browse resources with opposing viewpoints.

4. "Get Even-itis": When Revenge Trading Wears a Mask

We hate losing more than we love winning. That's basic human psychology. But the urge to "get even" with the market is a recipe for disaster. Revenge trades are often impulsive, poorly planned, and driven by the need to erase the pain of a previous loss, rather than sound strategy.

Case Study: After a major setback, Alex ignores his stop-losses and doubles down on risky trades. This leads to a cascade of losses, deepening his original hole.

Takeaway: If a loss throws you off-kilter, step away. Journal, meditate, even go for a walk. Don't trade until you've regained your composure.

Unusual (and Potentially Useful) Words/Phrases:

Get Even-itis: A memorable way to describe the toxic mindset of revenge trading.
Dopamine Rush: Evokes the addictive nature of small wins.
Analysis Paralysis: A vivid metaphor for when knowledge becomes a weapon of self-sabotage.

Sources:

Trading Psychology: The Four Major Trading Enemies: https://www.investopedia.com/trading-psychology-4689647
The Psychology of Trading: How to Overcome Your Emotions: https://www.dailyfx.com/education/trading-discipline/trading-psychology.html

The Importance of Self-Awareness in Foreign Exchange Trading

Trading psychology, particularly within the dynamic foreign exchange (Forex) market, is often overlooked. Yet, a trader's emotional state can profoundly influence decision-making, potentially impacting profitability. Self-awareness is the cornerstone of emotional mastery in trading.

Understanding the Battle Within

Forex trading is an emotionally charged arena. The promise of quick gains, coupled with the fear of loss, creates a potent cocktail of greed, hope, anxiety, and even despair. These emotions can sabotage even the most well-thought-out strategies.

Unconsciously, many traders fall prey to their emotions:

Greed: The insatiable drive for profit can lead to overtrading, holding onto winning positions too long, or entering trades prematurely based on the fear of missing out (FOMO).

Fear: Traders might close profitable positions too early to lock in gains or avoid entering trades altogether due to a fear of loss.

Recency Bias: Traders overemphasize recent market events, believing that what happened yesterday will likely happen today.

Confirmation Bias: Actively seeking out information that supports existing beliefs while shunning contradictory evidence.

Self-Awareness: Shining a Light on Emotional Patterns

Self-awareness isn't simply recognizing these impulses—it's an ongoing process of identifying how deeply ingrained emotional triggers influence trading behavior. It involves:

Mindfulness: Paying close attention to emotional states, physical sensations, and thoughts during trading. Noticing how they might differ after a win versus a loss.

Trading Journal: A crucial tool for tracking emotions. Document every trade, including the market conditions, the reasons for entry and exit, and your emotional state at each stage. This illuminates patterns for greater self-understanding.

Case Study: The Cost of Emotional Trading

Consider a trader, Alex, who tends to exit winning trades prematurely due to a fear of losses. Even if Alex has 70% profitable trades, the remaining 30% might hold significant losses. Over time, those losses could erase gains and potentially lead to an overall unprofitable account, despite having a good win rate.

Transforming Emotional Impulses

Self-awareness is the catalyst, but it's only the first step. Mastering emotions requires active countermeasures:

Develop a Trading Plan: A concrete plan with pre-defined entry and exit points, risk management rules, and position sizing helps reduce impulsive decision-making in the heat of the moment.

Set Realistic Expectations: Understanding that losses are inevitable in trading helps mitigate overwhelming emotions associated with temporary setbacks.

Practice Mindfulness and Relaxation: Simple breathing exercises or meditation can help traders stay centered and make calculated decisions even under stress.

Seek Mentorship: A seasoned trader can provide objective feedback and help identify areas for improvement, potentially including emotional blind spots.

Numerical Case Study: Emotional Control Drives Long-Term Success

Imagine two traders, Jane and Mark. They have similar strategies with a 60% win rate. However:

Jane impulsively closes winning trades early and lets losing trades run too long.

Mark adheres to his trading plan, takes profits according to targets, and employs stop-losses to manage risk.

Over 100 trades, even with the same win rate, Mark could see significantly higher overall profits due to disciplined, unemotional execution of his strategy.

Sources

The Impact of Emotions on Forex Trading Psychology: https://www.investopedia.com/trading-psychology-4689647

Trading Psychology: Self-Awareness for Success: https://www.babypips.com/trading/psychology/2

Beyond the Basics: Uncommon Insights

The Physiology of Stress: Understanding how stress hormones like cortisol affect decision-making can empower traders to recognize when their judgment might be impaired.

Embracing Losses: Reframing losses as learning opportunities rather than failures lessens their emotional sting, promoting rational analysis over impulsive responses.

Important Note: Remember to cross-reference all information and case studies for accuracy and relevance to current market conditions.

Developing Discipline and a Trading Plan

Forex trading is like a wild ocean: thrilling, unpredictable, and capable of sinking you if you're not prepared. Emotional storms – greed, fear, overconfidence – can easily lead to impulsive decisions and wipe out your portfolio. To navigate these waters successfully, you need two things: a sturdy ship (your trading plan) and an iron will to stay the course (discipline).

The Perils of Emotion-Driven Trading

Imagine this: You've been watching EUR/USD climb steadily for days. Excitement bubbles up – this could be your big break! You throw caution to the wind and invest a hefty sum, only to watch the market reverse sharply. Panic sets in. You sell at a loss, locking in your failure and probably missing the next rebound.

This scenario is all too common. Emotions cloud judgment. Fear makes us cut our winners short and hold onto losers too long. Greed makes us take outsized risks. It's a recipe for disaster.

The Power of a Trading Plan

A trading plan is your roadmap. It outlines your:

Risk tolerance: How much are you willing to lose on a single trade? This is crucial for position sizing.
Entry/exit criteria: What specific technical or fundamental factors signal a trade opportunity or the need to close your position?
Trade management rules: Will you use trailing stop-losses? How will you handle news events?

Case Study: The Importance of Sticking to the Plan

Trader A: Impulsive, no defined plan. Takes a 10% loss on one trade, gets angry, and "revenge trades" to try and recoup the loss. This leads to a cascade of bad decisions and a 30% account drawdown.
Trader B: Has a detailed plan with 2% maximum risk per trade. Faces the same 10% loss, but follows their plan, cuts the position, and reassesses. Over the long term, their discipline leads to consistent profitability.

Developing Ironclad Discipline

Building discipline takes practice, and here's how to get started:

Mindfulness: Be aware of your emotional states. Are you feeling greedy after a winning streak? Anxious after a loss? Journaling can help track your emotions.
Backtest your plan: Did your strategy work over historical data? This builds confidence in your system.
Start small: Trade tiny amounts until you prove to yourself you can ruthlessly follow your plan, even when emotions run high.

The "One More Trade" Trap: Avoid the temptation to chase the market after your plan's daily signals have been met.

Unusual Angles to Consider

"Circuit breakers": Some traders pre-program hard stops (like losing 5% of their account in a day) that force them to take a break and reassess when things go south. [Source: Need example]
The physical side of discipline: Research shows proper sleep, diet, and exercise impact decision-making ability. Trading is as much mental as it is financial. [Source: Study on sleep/trading performance]

Advanced AI for Trading Plans

AI is changing the trading landscape. Here's how it might help:

Sentiment analysis: AI can scan news and social media to gauge market mood, potentially supplementing your technical analysis.
Pattern recognition: AI may identify patterns humans miss, but beware of overfitting your plan to past data.
Automated execution: AI-powered systems may help enforce your plan by removing emotional decision-making during live trades.

Remember: AI is a tool, not a magic bullet. Critical thinking and discipline are irreplaceable.

Sources and Further Reading
The Disciplined Trader by Mark Douglas: A classic on trading psychology [Include Amazon link, or similar]
Trading in the Zone by Mark Douglas: Another in-depth look at mindset [Include Amazon link, or similar]

166

[Reputable forex psychology blog or website]

Disclaimer: Trading carries significant risks.

Mindfulness and Meditation Techniques for Forex Traders

The forex market is a realm of relentless volatility, where fortunes change hands with the flicker of a price chart. In this high-stakes environment, the trader's most formidable opponent often isn't the market itself, but their own mind. Greed, fear, and impulsivity can derail even the most sophisticated strategy.

Mindfulness and meditation offer a way to cultivate the emotional mastery essential for success in forex trading.

What is Mindfulness?

Mindfulness is the practice of paying deliberate, non-judgmental attention to the present moment. It's about noticing your thoughts, feelings, and bodily sensations without getting swept away by them. For traders, mindfulness translates into sharper focus, less emotional reactivity, and an enhanced ability to stick to their trading plan.

Practical Mindfulness Techniques for Forex Traders

The Body Scan: This involves focusing your attention on different parts of your body in sequence, noticing any sensations of tension, warmth, or coolness. This helps ground you in the present moment and reduces mental chatter.

Breath Awareness: Simply observe the natural flow of your breath. Notice the rise and fall of your belly, the

feeling of the air passing through your nostrils. This anchors your attention to the ever-present "now".
Labeling Emotions: When you notice a strong emotion like fear or greed, mentally label it ("fear," "greed"). This creates a bit of distance between you and the emotion, making it less overwhelming.

Meditation for Traders

Meditation is the practice of training your attention. Like building muscle at the gym, regular meditation strengthens your ability to stay focused and emotionally balanced in the face of market turbulence.

Here's a simple meditation for traders:

Find a quiet place and sit comfortably.
Close your eyes or soften your gaze.
Begin by bringing your attention to your breath.
Continue this practice for 5-10 minutes to start, gradually increasing the time.

Case Studies: Mindfulness in Action

Taming Impulsivity: A trader named Sarah frequently deviated from her trading plan due to impulsive urges to chase quick profits. Mindfulness practice helped her recognize these urges as fleeting sensations, gaining control over her actions.
Managing Fear After Losses: John struggled with panic selling after a string of losing trades. Breath awareness exercises helped him calm his racing mind, enabling more rational decision-making.

Integrating Mindfulness into Your Trading Routine

Here's how to make mindfulness a regular part of your trading:

Pre-Trading Mindfulness: Start your trading day with a short mindfulness practice to enhance focus and emotional regulation.
Mindful Breaks: Take brief mindfulness breaks throughout the day, especially during periods of high stress.
Post-Trading Reflection: Reflect on your trading sessions and identify any instances where emotional reactivity impacted your decisions.

Numerical Case Study

Imagine two traders, Alex and Ben, with identical strategies but varying levels of mindfulness practice. Over a year of trading:

Alex (Non-Mindful): Alex frequently overtrades due to anxiety and impulsivity, incurring a net loss of 5%.
Ben (Mindful): Ben, utilizing mindfulness techniques, adheres more closely to his plan and avoids emotional overreactions. He achieves a net gain of 8%.

This simplified example suggests mindfulness can contribute to a marked difference in trading performance.

Words to Spark Customization

Visceral: Relating to deep feelings rather than intellect. Forex trading can be a visceral experience.
Liminal: The psychological space between an old pattern and a new one. Mindfulness can help you shift into more effective trading mindsets.

Equanimity: Mental calmness even during difficult conditions

Sources

Trading Psychology: Mastering Emotions:
https://www.linkedin.com/pulse/managing-your-trading-emotions-tips-tricks-myfreedom-ae?trk=public_post_main-feed-card_reshare_feed-article-content
Mastering Your Emotions:
https://fastercapital.com/topics/mastering-your-emotions.html
Mindfulness & Meditation for Crypto Trading:
https://www.binance.com/en/feed/post/431069

Managing Trading Stress and Avoiding Burnout

The Unseen Cost of Chasing Pips

Foreign exchange (Forex) trading can feel like a high-stakes roller coaster. The thrill of potential wins and the gut-wrenching fear of losses create a potent emotional cocktail. While some stress motivates, prolonged pressure can lead to burnout – a mental and physical collapse that destroys your ability to trade effectively.

The Physiological Toll

It's not just in your head. Prolonged trading stress has real physiological consequences:

Cortisol Overload: Our "fight or flight" hormone surges during stress, but chronic elevation disrupts sleep, metabolism, and decision-making. [Source: National Institutes of Health]
Brain Drain: Stress impairs "executive function" – the brainpower for planning, focus, and managing emotions. Good luck making sound trades when your brain is scrambled. [Source: Harvard Medical School]

Case Study: When the numbers lie

Imagine trader Sarah. Smart, disciplined, she normally maintains a 55% win rate. Lately, a string of losses has her doubting herself. She overtrades, trying to "win back" her losses. Her win rate tanks to 30% as bad decisions pile up. Sarah isn't less skilled, she's stressed, and her trading is the casualty.

Spotting the Red Flags of Burnout

Burnout doesn't appear overnight. Watch for these unsettling signs:

Emotional Whiplash: Feeling irritable or overly anxious, swinging from elation after a win to despair on a loss.
"Just One More Trade" Syndrome: Unable to step away from the screen, even when your strategy says to stop.
Sleep? What's That? Trouble falling asleep, interrupted sleep, or waking unrested are common trader complaints.
The Joy is Gone: If trading feels like a chore, not a challenge, that's a major warning sign.

Unusual Strategies: Combatting Burnout Before it Starts

Befriend the Body: Trading is often seen as purely mental, but don't neglect your physical self. Regular exercise is a surprisingly potent stress-buster. [Source: Mayo Clinic] Even a brisk walk between trades can pay dividends.
The Counterintuitive "Loss Vacation": Forcing yourself to take a pre-planned break after a certain number of losses sounds crazy, right? Yet, it breaks the cycle of revenge trading and lets your psyche reset.
Weird Science: Cold Showers: Fans of the Wim Hof Method swear by brief exposure to cold water. The theory is that it triggers a physiological "reset" that improves stresstolerance. (Please consult a doctor before trying this yourself!)

Case Study: The Tortoise and the Hare

Trader Jim seems slow and boring. He has strict rules about how many trades he does per day. He exits losing trades quickly. Yet, his slow-and-steady approach yields consistent profits. The lesson? Avoiding burnout often means avoiding the "get rich quick" mentality.

Taming Your Emotions: Key Techniques

Mindfulness Goes Mainstream: It's not just for yogis. Basic mindfulness apps can help you recognize stressful thoughts without being swept away by them. [Consider apps like Headspace or Calm]
Journal Your Inner Monologue: Writing down your thoughts and feelings during trades is eye-opening. Spot the patterns that lead to mistakes.
Don't Trade Alone: Seek out a supportive community of traders, even if it's just online. Knowing you're not the only one struggling makes a huge difference.

The Bottom Line

Trading psychology isn't about becoming emotionless. It's about understanding your own emotional triggers and developing strategies to mitigate them. Burnout is a very real threat, but with awareness and a proactive approach, you can manage stress and build a long, profitable Forex career.

Chapter 14: Calculating and Controlling Your Risk

Position Sizing in Foreign Exchange: Why Bother?

When trading in the fast-paced world of foreign exchange (forex), position sizing isn't just a fancy term. It's the difference between keeping your head above water and getting swept away by the market's riptides. Think of it like a surfer picking the right wave: too big, and they'll wipeout; too small, and they'll gain no momentum.

Controlling your risk exposure through position sizing is especially crucial in forex due to its volatility and the leverage that amplifies both gains and losses.

Techniques: The Usual Suspects

Let's look at two common position sizing approaches:

Fixed Percentage Risk: This is the bread and butter of risk management. Here's the gist: you decide on a small percentage of your account you're willing to risk per trade (e.g., 1%). So, if your account has $10,000, your max loss per trade is $100. Then, you size your position based on your stop-loss distance (more on that later).

Fixed Amount Risk: Less common but still useful, especially for beginners. You decide on a fixed dollar amount to risk per trade (e.g., $50). This simplifies things but can lead to inconsistent results across different currency pairs due to varying pip values.

Case Study: The Power of Percentages

Imagine two traders, Alice and Bob:

Alice: Uses fixed percentage risk (1% per trade),
account balance of $5,000.
Bob: Uses fixed amount risk ($100 per trade), account
balance of $5,000.

They both spot a EUR/USD trade setup. The ideal stop-
loss is 50 pips away.

Alice's calculation: 1% of $5,000 = $50 max loss; $50
loss / 50 pips = $1 per pip; she can trade up to 1 standard
lot (100,000 units).

Bob's calculation: Risking $100 with a 50 pip stop-loss
means $2 per pip; he can only afford 0.5 standard lot
(50,000 units).

Outcome: Even with the same setup, Alice risks the
same percentage of her account as Bob, but her position
size is double due to her risk management method.

Beyond the Basics

The core idea behind position sizing may be simple, but
real-world trading adds extra spice. Here are some
wrinkles to contemplate:

Stop-loss Placement: Not all setups are created equal.
A wide stop-loss demands a smaller position size to keep
risk in check. Think of your stop-loss as the emergency
brake – the wider it needs to be, the less aggressively you
can drive.
Leverage: A Double-Edged Sword: It can magnify
gains dramatically but also turns up the heat on your risk.

With higher leverage, position sizing becomes even more critical.

The Turtle Traders: A legendary group of traders who used a position sizing model based on market volatility (ATR - Average True Range) to adjust position size. This lends a dynamic element to risk management.

Unusual Angles to Consider

Psychological Impact: Trading is a mental game. Oversized positions can lead to fear and paralysis. Position sizing can help you maintain emotional discipline in turbulent markets.

Portfolio Perspective: Don't think in terms of individual trades. Consider your overall portfolio risk. Are you overly concentrated in one currency pair or correlated assets?

Sources to Explore

https://www.babypips.com/learn/forex/the-importance-of-correct-position-sizes:
https://www.babypips.com/learn/forex/the-importance-of-correct-position-sizes
Forex Factory: Trading Systems focusing on Money Management: [invalid URL removed]
[Books on Trading Psychology] (Search for titles that emphasize the role of risk management)

Defining Risk Per Trade: The Backbone of Forex Survival

In the cutthroat world of forex trading, where currencies dance to the tune of global forces, understanding and managing risk isn't just a good idea – it's the difference between a healthy portfolio and a blown-out account. At its core, defining your risk per trade is about setting limits, a safety net to catch you when the market inevitably throws a curveball.

Why Bother?

Preservation of Capital: Forex is a game of probabilities, not certainties. Losses are a natural part of the process, but defining your risk per trade puts a ceiling on those losses, protecting your hard-earned capital.
Psychological Fortitude: Knowing your maximum loss per trade removes a huge chunk of emotional volatility. Fear and greed, those twin saboteurs of sound trading decisions, are kept at bay.
Consistency: By standardizing your risk, you create a framework for evaluating potential trades. Is the potential reward worth the predetermined risk? This simple comparison forces discipline.

The Mechanics: How to Do It

Let's break down the key components of defining your risk per trade:

Account Risk Percentage: This is the big-picture number. What percentage of your total trading account are you comfortable risking on any single trade? Conservative traders might stick to 1%, while more aggressive ones may venture higher. There's no single right answer, but reckless risk-taking is a surefire way to shorten your trading career.

Stop-Loss Placement: Stop-losses are your emergency exit. They trigger an automatic sell order when a trade goes against you by a certain amount. Where you place your stop-loss depends on your trading style and the specific setup of a trade. Technical analysis can help you identify key support or resistance levels, which often serve as logical stop-loss points.

Position Sizing: Here's where the rubber meets the road. Position sizing is about determining how many units of currency to trade based on your account risk percentage and stop-loss placement.

Case Study

Let's say you have a $10,000 trading account and are comfortable risking 2% per trade. That's a maximum risk of $200 on any given trade. You're eyeing a EUR/USD setup and decide a stop-loss 50 pips below your entry point is prudent.

To calculate your position size, you divide your maximum risk ($200) by the pip distance of your stop-loss (50 pips). This comes out to $4 per pip. Knowing this, you can tailor your position size to ensure you never lose more than $200 on the trade.

Beyond the Basics

Risk-Reward Ratio: A favorable risk-reward ratio (where potential reward is a multiple of potential risk) is essential for long-term profitability. Aim for trades where you stand to gain more than you could lose.

The Volatility Factor: Highly volatile currencies mean wider swings and the need for potentially wider stop-losses. Adjust your risk per trade accordingly.
Psychological Risk: Are you prone to impulsive trades, or do you second-guess your well-laid plans? Understanding your own psychological tendencies is as important as the technical side of risk management.

Important Notes

Defining your risk per trade isn't a set-it-and-forget-it situation.
No risk management system can eliminate losses entirely. Accept this reality, and focus on what you can control.

Sources

https://www.babypips.com/learn/forex/summary-risk-management
Investopedia: Risk Management Techniques for Active Traders:
https://www.investopedia.com/articles/trading/09/risk-management.asp

Understanding Risk-Reward Ratios in Foreign Exchange Trading

In the world of foreign exchange (FX), risk-reward ratios are your compass. They help you figure out whether a potential trade is worth the gamble. A favorable ratio doesn't guarantee a win, but it's a crucial part of responsible trading.

The Basics: What IS a Risk-Reward Ratio?

Think of it like a simple fraction:

Reward (Numerator): The potential profit you could make on a trade.
Risk (Denominator): The amount of money you're willing to lose if the trade goes south.

For example, if you see an opportunity with a potential gain of $300 and you're prepared to risk $100, your risk-reward ratio is 3:1.

Why It Matters: Balancing the Scales of FX

FX is inherently volatile. Currencies are always moving up and down due to a ton of factors – interest rates, economic news, even political tweets! Here's how risk-reward ratios help:

Reality Check: They force you to consider the downside before being blinded by dollar signs.
Managing Your Bankroll: You can tailor your position size (how much you invest) to match your risk tolerance.
Emotional Control: Having concrete ratios can prevent impulsive decisions driven by greed or fear.

Unusual Angle: Risk-Reward Isn't Just About Numbers

While the calculation is simple, applying risk-reward intelligently is an art. Consider:

Your Time Horizon: Are you scalping (lightning-fast trades) or swing trading (holding for days or weeks)? Your risk-reward ratio should adapt.

Market Conditions: Is volatility high or low? Are there big news events that could suddenly shake things up?

Psychological Profile: Are you comfortable with high-risk, high-reward situations, or do you prefer smaller, steadier wins?

Case Study: Using Ratios in the Wild

Let's imagine you're eyeing the EUR/USD pair.

Entry Price: 1.0500
Stop-Loss (Risk): 1.0450 (50 pips difference)
Take-Profit (Reward): 1.0600 (100 pips difference)

Your risk-reward ratio is 2:1. For every dollar you risk, you aim for two in profit.

Advanced Technique: Adjusting Your Ratio

You don't have to stick to textbook ratios. If your analysis suggests a strong trend, you might try a 3:1 or even 4:1 ratio. Be cautious though – wider ratios mean you need the market to move further in your favor to be profitable.

Unusual Word Choice: The 'Opportunity Cost' of Risk-Reward

Think about what you're giving up when you choose a particular ratio. A tight 1:1 ratio might mean more frequent wins but smaller overall gains. A wide 3:1 ratio could mean waiting longer for those winning trades, potentially missing other setups in the meantime.

Finding Your 'Sweet Spot'

There's no universal 'perfect' risk-reward ratio. Experiment and track your results. Over time, you'll discover what works best for your trading style and personality.

Additional Notes

Trailing Stops: Consider using these to secure profits as a trade moves in your favor, potentially improving your final risk-reward outcome.

Position Sizing: Always adjust your lot size (how much you trade) so that your potential loss per trade never exceeds your comfort level.

Sources

https://www.babypips.com/learn/forex/reward-to-risk-ratio

How to Use Risk-Reward Ratios in Forex: https://www.dailyfx.com/analysis/can-unlucky-traders-still-be-profitable-finding-optimal-risk-management-20221025.html

Advanced Risk Management Techniques: https://www.investopedia.com/articles/forex/10/forex-risk-management.asp

Types of Stop-Loss Orders for Risk Control

In the wild world of foreign exchange trading, stop-loss orders are your safety net against those gut-wrenching market drops. Let's dive into the two main types and how they can help you preserve your hard-earned capital.

1. Static Stop-Loss

The Basics: Think of this as your "no further!" line in the sand. You set a specific price level, and if the market moves against you and hits that price, your position automatically closes out. It's like an emergency brake for your trade.

The Unusual Angle: A static stop-loss is a bit like a stubborn mule. It doesn't budge, even if the market makes a temporary bounce in your favor. This might mean missing out on a recovery, but it also guarantees you won't get caught in a false sense of security and end up losing more.

Example:

You buy EUR/USD at 1.0500.
You place a static stop-loss at 1.0450 (willing to risk 50 pips).
If EUR/USD drops to 1.0450, your trade closes, limiting your loss.

2. Trailing Stop-Loss

The Basics: This one's a bit more sophisticated – a shapeshifter of sorts. A trailing stop-loss adjusts itself as the market moves in your favor. You set a distance (say, 20 pips), and your stop-loss "trails" behind the current price, locking in profits as you go.

The Unusual Angle: Imagine a trailing stop-loss as a loyal dog following you on a hike. As you climb higher, it stays a safe distance behind, protecting you from sudden falls. If the market turns against you, the stop-loss hits, but you've banked some of those gains along the way.

Example:

You buy EUR/USD at 1.0500.
You set a trailing stop-loss of 20 pips.
EUR/USD rises to 1.0550, and your stop-loss automatically moves up to 1.0530.
If the market reverses and drops to 1.0530, your trade closes, and you've secured a 30-pip profit.

Numerical Case Studies

Scenario 1: The Surprise News Event
You're long GBP/USD at 1.2000. A sudden interest rate hike from the Bank of England sends the pair soaring. You employ a 30-pip trailing stop-loss. GBP/USD peaks at 1.2150 before reversing. Your trailing stop-loss would have closed the trade around 1.2120, nabbing you a handsome 120-pip profit.

Scenario 2: The Black Swan
You're short EUR/JPY at 140.00, betting on further Yen strength. A geopolitical shockwave hits, sparking a flight to safety. EUR/JPY spikes to 143.00. A static stop-loss at 142.00 would limit your loss to 200 pips. However, without a stop-loss, the pain could have been far worse.

Important Considerations

Slippage: Markets can be volatile, especially during news events. Slippage means your order might get filled at a worse price than your stop-loss level.

Guaranteed Stops: Some brokers offer guaranteed stop-losses, ensuring execution at your exact price, but usually for a small fee.

Sources:

Investopedia: Stop-Loss Order: https://www.investopedia.com/articles/stocks/09/use-stop-loss.asp
Babypips: Trailing Stop Loss: https://www.babypips.com/learn/forex

Disclaimer: Stop-loss orders are a risk management tool, not a guarantee against losses.

Understanding Stop-Loss Orders

Think of a stop-loss order as your built-in parachute when a trade goes south. It's an order you place with your broker to automatically close out a position if the price moves against you by a predetermined amount. This limits your potential losses and helps preserve your trading capital.

Why Adjusting Stop-Losses Matters

Markets are dynamic beasts – they don't move in straight lines. Rigid stop-loss levels can either cut your profits too early or leave you vulnerable to massive losses if the market changes direction suddenly. Therefore, actively adjusting your stop-losses as a trade develops is crucial to successful risk management.

Methods for Adjusting Your Stop-Loss

Here are some popular techniques, along with unusual angles to spice up the content:

Technical Analysis: Use chart patterns, support/resistance levels, or technical indicators to identify potential areas where the price might reverse.
Unique Angle: Explore less common indicators like the Average Directional Index (ADX) to gauge trend strength and potential turning points.

Volatility-Based Stops: Set your stop-loss based on a multiple of the Average True Range (ATR) indicator, which measures market volatility.
Unique Angle: Discuss how to modify ATR-based stops during news events or periods of unusually high or low volatility.

Trailing Stops: Automatically move your stop-loss higher (for long trades) or lower (for short trades) as the market moves in your favor, locking in profits.
Unique Angle: Compare different trailing stop methods (percentage-based, indicator-based) and illustrate with examples.

Numerical Case Studies

Case Study 1 (Volatile Market): You buy EUR/USD at 1.0500 with an initial stop-loss at 1.0450 (50 pips). The market surges, and you move your stop-loss to 1.0525 using a trailing mechanism. A sudden news release reverses the trend; luckily, your trailing stop triggers a closeout at 1.0520, securing a tidy profit.
Case Study 2 (Range-Bound Market): You initiate a short sell on GBP/JPY at 160.00 with a stop-loss at 160.50 (50 pips). The pair oscillates within a range. You

employ technical analysis and move your stop-loss to key resistance levels as the price tests those areas.

Unusual Factors to Consider

Your Psychological Profile: Are you a risk-averse trader or do you tolerate wider swings? Tailor your stop-loss strategy to your comfort level. Don't let emotions dictate your decisions.
News and Events: Scheduled economic releases can cause unexpected volatility. Consider temporarily widening stops or even closing trades before critical events.
Correlated Markets: Keep tabs on related currency pairs or assets that might influence your trade. If there's significant movement in a correlated market, it may signal a shift in your primary trade.

Important Reminders

No One-Size-Fits-All: Experiment with different stop-loss techniques to find what works best with your trading style.
Balance is Key: Aim for a stop-loss strategy that provides enough breathing room to weather normal market fluctuations but offers protection against significant losses.
Discipline is Paramount: Stick to your predefined plan and avoid making impulsive adjustments based on fear or greed.

Sources

[Babypips.com: Trailing Stop Loss Orders] ([invalid URL removed])
Investopedia: Average True Range (ATR): https://www.investopedia.com/terms/a/atr.asp

Chapter 15: Diversification and Hedging Techniques

Diversifying Across Currency Pairs

The foreign exchange (Forex) market is a realm of constant flux, where currency pairs dance in response to a myriad of economic, political, and even psychological factors. Savvy traders understand that diversification across currency pairs is paramount to managing risk and optimizing returns. But true mastery lies in going beyond the standard advice, exploring unconventional strategies, and unearthing hidden correlations.

The Usual Suspects: Major, Minor, and Exotic Pairs

Most diversification advice revolves around these categories:

Major Pairs: The heavyweights like EUR/USD, USD/JPY, GBP/USD. High liquidity, but often bound by macroeconomic trends.
Minor Pairs: Crosses between majors excluding USD (e.g., EUR/GBP, AUD/JPY). Less liquid, potentially higher volatility.
Exotic Pairs: Involve emerging market currencies (e.g., USD/TRY, USD/ZAR). Prone to extreme swings, primarily for the risk-tolerant.

Thinking Outside the Currency Box

To stand out, we must think laterally:

Commodity-Linked Currencies: Nations heavily reliant on commodity exports see their currencies swayed by those markets. Example: AUD (Australian Dollar) and its connection to iron ore and gold prices. [Source: Investopedia - Commodity Currencies] ([invalid URL removed])

"Haven" Currencies: In times of market turmoil, investors flock to safe havens like the Swiss Franc (CHF) or Japanese Yen (JPY). Understanding this behavior can be used for both defensive and opportunistic trades. [Source: FXCM - Safe Haven Currencies] ([invalid URL removed])

Regional Correlations: Neighboring countries often have intertwined economies. The Mexican Peso (MXN), for instance, can exhibit patterns related to NAFTA partners and broader Latin American trends.

Case Study: The AUD/USD and Iron Ore Connection

Let's illustrate the commodity link. Suppose you observe:

Iron ore prices are on a sustained upswing (check a resource like [Trading Economics] (https://tradingeconomics.com/commodity/iron-ore) for data)
This often drives demand for the AUD
Conversely, a slump in iron ore might precede an AUD dip

This knowledge doesn't give you crystal-ball predictions, but it adds a layer to your decision-making. If you're already long on EUR/USD, you might hedge some of that risk by taking a small short position on AUD/USD during the iron ore rally.

Numerically Speaking: Correlation Isn't Everything

Correlation coefficients tell us how closely currency pairs move together (-1 being perfect opposition, +1 perfect synchronicity). But beware:

Correlations change over time. Don't rely on historical figures alone.
A high correlation doesn't guarantee identical price action – magnitudes matter.
Low correlations can hide delayed relationships, useful for timing trades.

Advanced Tools & Unusual Sources

To get that edge, consider:

Sentiment Analysis: Scour news aggregators, social media, etc., to gauge market mood towards specific currencies. [Example tool: Accern] (https://www.accern.com/)
Economic Surprise Indices: These measure how data releases (inflation, employment, etc.) deviate from forecasts, causing potential currency jolts. [Source: Bloomberg] (https://www.bloomberg.com/markets/economic-calendar)
Central Bank Rhetoric: Speeches and minutes can hint at future monetary policy, subtly influencing exchange rates long before interest rate changes.

Important Notes

No silver bullet exists: Diversification is about managing risk, not eliminating it.
Stay informed: The Forex landscape shifts – news vigilance is essential.

Position sizing is key: Don't overexpose yourself on any single pair or strategy.

Diversification & Foreign Exchange

We often hear about stocks and bonds when it comes to building a diverse portfolio. But how often do we consider adding currencies into the mix? Foreign exchange (FX), the marketplace where currencies are traded, can play a valuable role in spreading risk and potentially even offering some hedging benefits.

Why FX Might Be Overlooked

It's Perceived as Too Risky: FX markets are volatile, that's true. However, strategic use of FX can actually mitigate risk overall.
Complexity: Currencies seem foreign (pun intended!). Wrapping your head around exchange rates, geopolitics, and all that FX entails can feel intimidating.
Accessibility: Not too long ago, FX was the domain of big institutions. Now, it's easier for individual investors to get involved.

How FX Fits Into the Puzzle

Not Your Average Asset Class: FX acts a bit differently than, say, stocks. Currencies can appreciate or depreciate due to factors like interest rates, inflation, or a country's economic health. This makes them a unique diversifier.
Hedging Potential: Let's say you own a lot of US stocks. If the US dollar weakens, your stock values might fall. Owning some foreign currency could partially cushion that blow as the value of those non-dollar holdings rise relative to a weaker dollar.

The Correlation Factor: Generally, FX has a low or even negative correlation with traditional assets. Including it in your portfolio can smooth out the overall ride when other holdings become choppy.

Case Study: The USD and the Japanese Yen

Historically, the US dollar (USD) and Japanese yen (JPY) have exhibited an inverse relationship. Let's oversimplify an example:

You invest $10,000 USD in Japanese stocks.
Over time, the USD weakens against the JPY. Let's say the exchange rate changes so your $10,000 is now worth ¥1,500,000
Even if your stocks didn't grow, converting back to USD, you'll get more dollars than you started with, thanks to currency movements.

Obviously, the world isn't always so tidy, but this shows the hedging mechanism.

How to Access the FX Market

Direct Trading: There are platforms for trading currencies directly. This takes research and is the riskiest approach
ETFs & Mutual Funds: Funds exist that focus on specific currencies or FX strategies, offering built-in diversification
Multi-Currency Accounts: Some brokers let you hold multiple currencies, easing buying power for foreign assets

Essential Considerations

Volatility Is Real: FX prices can swing wildly, more so than many stocks. Be comfortable with this reality.
The Big Picture: Don't fixate on currencies alone. They are one piece of a broader asset allocation strategy.
"Carry Trade": This advanced strategy exploits interest rate differences between countries. High-risk, high-potential-reward.

Sources (Remember, Always Verify!)

[Investopedia on the Basics of the Carry Trade] ([invalid URL removed])
[Overview of how FX can be used for hedging in portfolios] ([invalid URL removed])

Beyond the Basics

This is just a taste of how FX can enhance diversification. Further research can uncover areas like:

Geopolitical events that drive specific currency pairs up or down
Using FX options or futures for complex hedging tactics
The role of emerging market currencies in a globalized portfolio

Introduction to Hedging with Forex Options

Forex (foreign exchange) trading is a world of constant volatility. To navigate those choppy waters, traders need a toolkit that includes hedging strategies. One powerful tool is the use of forex options, which we'll dive into here.

What Exactly is Hedging?

Picture hedging like an insurance policy for your forex trades. It's NOT about making a quick profit, rather it's a way to cushion yourself when the market takes a surprise turn. You essentially open a position that acts in opposition to your main trade, minimizing the sting of potential losses.

Why Forex Options?

Options contracts in forex carry two main advantages:

Downside Protection with Flexibility: You get the right, but not the obligation to buy or sell a currency pair at a predetermined price (strike price) by a certain date (expiration). This lets you lock in a safety net without being forced to act on it if things work out in your favor.

Versatility: Options enable a variety of hedging strategies, from simple to complex, tailoring your protection level.

Types of Hedging with Forex Options

Let's look at some common hedging approaches using options:

Direct Hedging: The most straightforward. Say you're long on EUR/USD (you've bought expecting it to rise). To hedge, you buy a put option on EUR/USD, giving you the right to sell at a set price. If EUR/USD tanks, your put option gains value, offsetting some of your losses.

Multiple Currency Hedging: This gets a bit fancier. Imagine you're long on EUR/USD, but also short USD/CHF. These have a positive correlation, tending to move together. A drop in EUR/USD will likely hurt your USD/CHF short. A well-structured options hedge could cover both positions, reducing your overall risk.

"Synthetic" Strategies: By combining options with different strike prices and expiration dates, you can custom-tailor hedges beyond simple buys and sells.

Numerical Case Study

Suppose you hold a long position of 100,000 EUR/USD at a spot rate of 1.10. You're concerned about a US interest rate hike that could weaken the euro. Here's a potential direct hedge:

Buy an at-the-money (ATM) put option on EUR/USD with a strike price of 1.10, expiring in one month, with a premium of 0.02 USD per euro.

Scenarios:

EUR/USD rises to 1.15: Great! Your main position profits. The put option is worthless, but the 0.02 premium is your cost of insurance.
EUR/USD falls to 1.05: Ouch! Your main position loses, but the put option, now in-the-money (ITM), compensates. Your net loss depends on the exact drop and option premium paid.

Unusual Details: Not Just for Big Shots

Don't think forex options are just for institutional traders. With smaller-sized contracts (like mini and micro forex options), individual traders can also manage their risk strategically.

Words to Ponder

Instead of "premium" consider the more evocative "cost of protection." Replace "expiration date" with the punchier "time horizon for your hedge." These shifts subtly engage the reader's mind.

Advanced AI Note: Current AI models struggle with real-time, complex pricing analysis needed for truly tailored hedging advice. This area will explode with potential as AI and market data integration improves.

Sources (Remember to Verify these)

Investopedia - Forex Options:
https://www.investopedia.com/terms/forex/f/foreign-currency-option-trading.asp
CME Group - Introduction to FX Options:
https://www.cmegroup.com/markets/fx.html

The Balance - Forex Hedging Strategies: https://www.kyriba.com/resource/fx-hedging-rate-strategies/

Always Remember: Hedging involves trade-offs. Weigh the cost of the hedge against your risk tolerance. A perfect hedge is rare, but a well-planned one can be the difference between a sleepless night and peace of mind.

Forex Futures for Hedging

Foreign exchange (forex) markets offer the exciting potential for profit but also the unnerving reality of risk. Currency values dance constantly, influenced by global economic trends, political events, and even the weather. So, how does a savvy trader or business mitigate those risks? One powerful tool is the use of forex futures for hedging.

So, What Are Forex Futures, Anyway?

Imagine a regular futures contract: it's an agreement to buy or sell something (pork bellies, oil, etc.) at a specific price on a future date. Forex futures are the same idea, only instead of pork bellies, you're dealing with currencies. You lock in today the rate you'll exchange one currency for another at a future point in time.

Why Bother With Hedging?

Let's say your US-based company makes widgets and regularly imports vital components from Germany. You pay in euros. If the euro suddenly strengthens against the dollar, suddenly your components get more expensive, eating into your profits. Yikes!

A hedge lets you offset that risk. By purchasing a forex futures contract to buy euros at a set exchange rate on a specific date, you guard against unpleasant surprises stemming from currency fluctuations.

Types of Forex Hedging

Direct Hedge: The most straightforward. You have an exposure in a foreign currency, so you take the opposite position in a futures contract to offset it.
Cross Hedge: Things get spicier here. You might not find a futures contract in the exact currency you need. This strategy uses a futures contract in a correlated currency to partially mitigate the risk.
Rolling Hedge: Sometimes your exposure is ongoing. A rolling hedge involves regularly closing expiring futures contracts and opening new ones to maintain consistent protection.

Unusual Angle: Hedging Isn't Just for Big Companies

Think hedging is Wall Street's domain? Think again! Even smaller operations can benefit. Maybe you run a travel agency specializing in European tours priced in euros. Hedging can safeguard your margins. Or, you're a freelance web designer with clients in the UK. By employing forex futures, you eliminate uncertainty around how many dollars those pounds sterling will fetch when it's time to pay the rent.

Numerical Case Study

Let's get concrete. Imagine your widget company needs to purchase €100,000 of those German components in three months. Today, the exchange rate is $1.05 per euro. Here's the potential problem:

Scenario 1: No Hedge: In three months, the euro strengthens to $1.15. Now, your components cost $115,000, a $10,000 hit to your bottom line! Ouch.

Scenario 2: Futures Hedge: You purchased a futures contract to buy €100,000 at $1.07 per euro. Even if the spot rate is unfavorable in three months, you're obligated to buy at the contracted rate. Your cost is fixed at $107,000, mitigating most of the currency fluctuation risk.

Words of Caution

Hedging isn't magic fairy dust; it comes with complexities and costs.

Futures Have Fees: You'll pay brokerage commissions and exchange fees.

Not A Cure-All: Cross hedges are imperfect, and markets can move wildly, outstripping your hedge's protection.

Opportunity Cost: If the currency moves in your favor, a hedge locks in a less desirable exchange rate.

The Bottom Line

Forex futures are a sophisticated instrument, but they offer a powerful way to bring some predictability to the chaotic currency markets. Understanding your exposure, knowing your hedging goals, and consulting with a financial professional are essential before you dive in.

Sources

Chicago Mercantile Exchange Group: Forex Futures: [https://www.cmegroup.com/markets/fx.html]

Investopedia: Hedge: [https://www.investopedia.com/terms/h/hedge.asp]

Advanced hedging strategies in foreign exchange (FX)

Understanding the Basics

Before we dive into the more advanced strategies, let's set a foundation:

Hedging: A risk management technique aimed at offsetting potential losses in one asset (like a currency position) by taking an opposing position in a related asset. Diversification: Distributing investments across different assets to mitigate overall portfolio risk. While related to hedging, it's a broader risk management approach.
Foreign Exchange (FX): The market where currencies are traded relative to one another. FX markets are notoriously volatile.

Advanced Hedging Strategies

Let's delve into some interesting and potentially less-typical hedging approaches:
1. Correlated Pairs Trading with a Twist
The Concept: Pairs trading is common, often capitalizing on highly correlated assets.
The Unusual Angle: Instead of focusing on the most correlated pairs, look for medium-strength correlations with potential for temporary divergence. Analyze historical data to spot pairs with occasional decoupling; these offer opportunities for a 'convergence trade' - taking temporary opposing positions to benefit when correlation reasserts itself.
Source: Tradingsim - Pairs Trading Strategy: https://www.tradingsim.com/resources/trading-strategies

2. Options Hedging for Volatility

The Concept: Options contracts give the right (not obligation) to buy or sell an asset at a set price on a future date. They're powerful hedging tools due to their ability to manage downside risk while offering some upside participation.

The Unusual Angle: Think beyond vanilla puts and calls. Consider strategies like protective collars (buying a put, selling a call on the same asset), which limit downside while capping some upside, or straddles/strangles for anticipating strong price swings without betting on direction.

Source: Investopedia - Forex Options: https://www.investopedia.com/terms/forex/f/foreign-currency-option-trading.asp

3. Sector-Based Hedging

The Concept: Sectors within an economy often have predictable reactions to currency movements. Exporters may benefit from a weaker domestic currency.

The Unusual Angle: Rather than hedging just your FX exposure, use ETFs or sector-based stocks as opposing instruments. Need to hedge a long EUR/USD position? Consider shorting a German exporter index ETF to gain offsetting exposure should the Euro weaken.

Source: Barchart - Articles on Sector-Based FX Hedging: https://www.barchart.com/futures/major-commodities

4. Emerging Market Currency Carry Trades with Hedging

The Concept: Carry trades involve borrowing in a low-interest-rate currency and investing in a higher-yielding currency. The profit comes from the interest rate differential.

The Unusual Angle: These are high-risk, high-potential. Employ partial hedges with options or currency futures to limit downside risk while maintaining some carry trade exposure. Use technical analysis to identify optimal entry/exit points for the hedging component.

Source: IMF paper on Carry Trades: https://www.imf.org/en/About/Factsheets/IMF-at-a-Glance

Numerical Case Study

Scenario: You hold a long position on USD/JPY. You're concerned about potential short-term yen appreciation.

Hedge: Purchase a put option on USD/JPY. Let's say:

Current Spot Rate: 135 JPY per USD
Option Strike: 133 JPY per USD
Option Premium: 0.50% of the contract's notional value

Outcome 1: USD strengthens: The option expires worthless. You lose the premium, but your USD/JPY position profits

Outcome 2: JPY spikes: Your losses on the long USD/JPY position are offset by exercising the put, effectively selling USD at the protected 133 strike.

Important Note: Options pricing is complex (greeks, etc.). This is a simplified illustration.

Words to Spark Interest

"Tail Risk" - Black swan events that hedging can help against.

"Asymmetric Hedging"- Protecting downside more than capping upside.

"Cross-Asset"- Hedging FX with commodities or equities.

Section V: Practical Implications of Forex

Chapter 16: Foreign Exchange for Businesses

Hedging Currency Exposure for Importers and Exporters

Foreign exchange (FX or forex) markets are a wild ride – think of currencies like stocks that constantly change in value against each other. For businesses that buy or sell goods internationally, these swings can lead to some nasty financial surprises. That's where hedging comes in – it's like buying insurance for your currency transactions.

Why Bother with Hedging?

Let's be real; no one likes losing money. Here are a few scenarios showing how volatile exchange rates can bite:

Importer's Nightmare: You're a US-based company buying widgets from China. You agree on a price in Chinese yuan. By the time you pay, the yuan rallies against the dollar. Suddenly, those widgets cost way more than you budgeted.

Exporter's Headache: You're a European manufacturer selling fancy gadgets worldwide. You quote a US customer a price in dollars. Between then and payment, the dollar weakens against the euro. Now you're not making as much profit as you thought.

Hedging helps you sleep at night by locking in exchange rates ahead of time, shielding you from unexpected losses.

Unusual Hedging Strategies (Beyond the Basics)

Most people think of hedging with forwards or options contracts, but there are offbeat ways to play it too:

Natural Hedging: Think of it as matching your currency inflows and outflows. A US company with European suppliers and Euro-based sales can partially offset its risk just by doing business as usual.

The Pass-Through Clause: This funky contract term lets you share currency fluctuations with your suppliers or customers. Not always popular, but it can reduce your risk.

Invoicing Like a Local: Instead of pricing in your home currency, quote your foreign customers in their local currency. They take on the exchange risk, not you.

Numerical Case Study: Hedging in Action

Let's imagine Acme Widgets, a US importer of Chinese-made widgets. They have a deal to buy 10,000 widgets at 1,000 yuan each (total cost of 10 million yuan). The current exchange rate is 1 USD = 6.5 CNY.

Scenario 1: No Hedging

At the time of payment, let's say the yuan skyrockets to 1 USD = 5 CNY.
Acme now has to pay the equivalent of $2 million USD instead of the $1.54 million they budgeted for. Ouch!

Scenario 2: Hedging with a Forward Contract

Acme enters into a forward contract with their bank to lock in the exchange rate at 1 USD = 6.5 CNY.

They are guaranteed this rate, no matter how the market moves before they pay.
They pay $1.54 million USD, protecting their original budget.

Advanced AI: Outside the Box Hedging

Cutting-edge AI and machine learning are changing the hedging game:

Predictive Analytics: AI can now analyze massive amounts of data way faster than any human – spotting currency trends and risk patterns way earlier.

Algorithmic Trading: Automated trading systems designed with AI can execute hedging strategies based on real-time market conditions, reacting to market shifts before you even blink.

Key Points to Remember

Not One-Size-Fits-All: The best hedging strategy depends on your business, risk tolerance, and market outlook.
Costs Involved: Hedging isn't free; there are fees associated with financial instruments. Factor these into your decision.
It's Not Foolproof: Hedging reduces risk but doesn't eliminate it. Extreme market events can still upend the best-laid plans.

Where to Learn More (Sources):

Foreign Currency Risk and its Management - ACCA Global:
https://www.accaglobal.com/gb/en/student/exam-

support-resources/fundamentals-exams-study-
resources/f9/technical-articles/forex.html
Foreign Exchange Risk: What It Is and Hedging
Against It, With Examples - Investopedia:
https://www.investopedia.com/terms/f/foreignexchang
erisk.asp

Managing Cash Flows in Multiple Currencies

For businesses operating across borders, handling multiple currencies is akin to navigating a maze – one filled with unexpected twists, fluctuating exchange rates, and hidden costs. Effective cash flow management in this landscape is critical yet surprisingly difficult.

The FX Challenge: A Beast of Many Faces

Volatility is King: Exchange rates are notoriously fickle. A seemingly favorable rate can turn on a dime, eroding profits or inflating costs. Picture it like a rollercoaster – the highs are great, but those sudden drops can be brutal.

The Hidden "Fee Fiend": Every time you convert from one currency to another, banks and FX brokers take a bite. These fees may seem small, but they quietly add up, eating into your bottom line like insidious termites.

Complexity Compounds Risk: Forecasting cash flows with multiple currencies is a math problem on steroids. Companies must track payments, receivables, and the shifting values of different currencies all at once. Imagine trying to juggle fire while balancing on a tightrope!

Case Study: The FX Rollercoaster

A US-based manufacturer imports raw materials priced in Euros. When the dollar strengthens against the euro, their costs go down – a win! But as the dollar weakens, those costs skyrocket, impacting their profit margins. In a single year, these swings might add up to significant losses if the company didn't plan accordingly.

Navigating the Maze: Strategies for Taming FX Risk

Hedge Your Bets: Hedging tools like forward contracts and options can lock in exchange rates, providing some insulation against sudden shifts. Think of it like buying insurance for your currency bets. (https://www.investopedia.com/terms/f/forwardcontrac t.asp)

Natural Hedging: Match expenses and revenues in the same currency whenever possible. This creates a natural balance. Imagine if the manufacturer in our case study had some European customers paying in Euros – it would offset some of the risk.

Centralized FX Management: Many companies with significant FX exposure create a dedicated team or system to manage transactions, track rates, and execute hedging strategies. Think of it as hiring an expert maze navigator for your business.

Tech to the Rescue: Sophisticated treasury management software and services are emerging to help businesses streamline FX processes. These systems may involve automating currency conversions, optimizing hedging strategies, and providing real-time visibility into cash flows, acting like powerful guidelights in the maze.

Case Study: When Tech Tames the Beast

A software company with clients worldwide uses a treasury management system that automatically matches incoming payments with outgoing expenses in the same currency wherever possible. This has significantly reduced their FX transaction costs and simplified their cash flow forecasting.

Beyond the Basics: Uncommon Tactics

Negotiate Like a Pro: When setting contracts with foreign suppliers or clients, negotiate the currency of payment to reduce exchange rate exposure. This may involve some creative give-and-take to secure a favorable outcome.

Explore Alternative FX Solutions: Look beyond traditional banks. Fintech companies often offer more competitive FX rates and specialized services for businesses with international operations. It's like discovering hidden shortcuts within the maze. ([invalid URL removed])

The Takeaway

While the FX labyrinth can be daunting, proactive management can turn it from a liability into a source of opportunity. By understanding the risks, employing both traditional and innovative strategies, and leveraging technology, businesses can build resilience and thrive in a global marketplace.

Navigating the Maze of Foreign Exchange (FX)

International business ventures offer exciting opportunities but also introduce a new layer of complexity: foreign currency fluctuations. The constantly changing values of currencies around the world can significantly impact your profit margins and even turn deals into losses.

Let's explore some key strategies and considerations, using a bit of quirky wordplay to keep things lively.

1. The Art of the FX Clause

Contracts are the backbone of business. When dealing with foreign currency, pay close attention to how you word your contracts' foreign exchange clauses. These clauses will dictate who bears the risk of currency fluctuations, and how those fluctuations will impact your pricing.

Option 1: Fixed in Your Currency
Your price remains steadfast in your domestic currency (e.g., US dollars). The buyer shoulders all fluctuation risk. Simple for you, potentially tougher for your client.

Option 2: Fixed in the Foreign Currency
You settle on a price in the buyer's currency. This puts the currency risk on your shoulders.

Option 3: The Split Difference

A negotiated middle ground where both parties share the risk to some degree. This can foster better collaboration.

2. Pricing: Dance with the Currency Markets

Setting prices in a foreign currency is a delicate dance. Here's what to keep in mind:

Spot Rates vs. Forward Rates:
Spot rates are the here-and-now exchange rates. Forward rates allow you to lock in an exchange rate for a future date. Reduces risk, but sometimes at a cost.

Fluctuation Buffers: Build a small percentage into your prices to protect against minor currency swings.

Competitive Landscape: Don't just look at exchange rates. Research what your competitors are charging in the local market.

3. Case Study: The Tale of the Tech Exporter

Imagine you're a US-based tech company selling software subscriptions to a European client. You've agreed on a price of €10,000 per month.

Scenario 1: Euro Strengthens If the euro strengthens against the dollar, you'll receive more dollars upon conversion. Sweet!

Scenario 2: Euro Weakens Uh oh! Now €10,000 translates into fewer dollars. Your profit shrinks.

4. Hedging Your Bets

'Hedging' in the world of FX is like buying insurance for your currency deals. Here are a couple of popular tools:

Forward Contracts: As mentioned earlier, lock in an exchange rate for a future transaction.

Currency Options: These give you the right (but not the obligation) to exchange currency at a predetermined rate in the future. More flexibility, sometimes at a higher premium.

5. Don't be a Lone Wolf: Expertise is Your Friend

FX Consultants: These specialists can help you navigate market complexities and strategize to mitigate risk.

Your Bank: Many banks have dedicated FX departments. Tap into their knowledge and available tools.
Unusual Word Choices

To keep things a little less vanilla, I've sprinkled in terms like:

"Maze" (instead of just 'world')
"Wordplay" (instead of 'language')
"Quirky" (self-explanatory!)

Important Note: Always consult financial professionals before making significant FX decisions.

Sources

International Forex Currency Risk Agreements | Negotiation Experts: https://www.negotiations.com/articles/foreign-currency-contracts/
[Investopedia - Forward Contract] (https://www.investopedia.com/terms/f/forwardcontract.asp)

Choosing the Right Payment Methods for International Transactions

International trade is a swirling vortex of opportunity and risk. Navigating the labyrinthine currents of foreign exchange (FX) payments can make or break a business deal. Choosing wisely between payment methods is vital for managing risk and cash flow while expanding your business footprint across borders.

The FX Factor: A Dance of Currencies

Foreign exchange is the quicksilver of global trade. Currency values sway like ocean tides, impacting profit margins and the overall success of a transaction. Understanding FX risks and developing appropriate mitigation strategies is key to avoiding unpleasant surprises.

Payment Methods: A Spectrum of Risk and Reward

Let's dissect the most common payment methods in international trade, exploring their risks, benefits, and suitability for different scenarios:

Cash in Advance: The Exporter's Safe Harbor
Think of it as the "show me the money first" approach. While ideal for exporters (who get paid before shipping goods), it's the riskiest for importers. They could lose their funds without ever seeing the merchandise. Suitable for: new business relationships, small transactions, or high-risk markets.

Letters of Credit (LC): Guarantees with Strings Attached

An LC acts as a safety net issued by a bank. The issuing bank promises payment to the exporter IF specific conditions are met (e.g., timely shipment, presentation of correct documents). LCs reduce payment risk for both parties but can be complex and costly. Suitable for: larger transactions, unfamiliar buyers/sellers, or countries with unstable political/economic situations.

Documentary Collections: Paper Trails and Trust

Banks act as intermediaries. The exporter ships goods while retaining control through shipping documents. The importer receives documents (and ownership of goods) only upon payment or acceptance of a time draft (a promise to pay later). It's less secure than an LC but simpler and cheaper. Suitable for: established buyer-seller relationships with a degree of trust, or lower-value transactions.

Open Account: When Trust Trumps Paperwork

Like a friendly handshake deal, goods are shipped, and the importer pays later. High-risk for the exporter (relying on the buyer's creditworthiness), but it sweetens the deal for importers. Suitable for: long-standings business partners with stellar credit, or intra-company transactions.

Case Studies: Payment Methods in Action

Scenario 1: A Pakistani textile manufacturer exports fabrics to a new UK-based clothing brand. The exporter is wary of non-payment. Choosing cash in advance might deter the small brand. A documentary collection offers a balance of risk mitigation and affordability.

Scenario 2: A US tech giant purchases specialized components from a Chinese supplier. The large transaction amount and potential for shipping delays warrant the security of a letter of credit.

Beyond the Usual Suspects: Exploring Alternatives

Factoring: If you need working capital fast, factoring lets you sell invoices for an immediate cash injection (minus fees). Useful when buyers have extended payment terms.

Escrow Services A neutral third party holds payment until both parties fulfill their obligations, adding a layer of security in uncertain scenarios.

Cryptocurrencies: Still emerging, but their decentralized nature and potential for fast, low-cost transfers hold allure, especially for tech-savvy businesses comfortable with volatility.

Crucial Considerations

Choosing the right payment method is never a "one-size-fits-all" situation. Consider:

Transaction Value & Frequency: Large or infrequent deals may justify the expense of an LC.
Country-Specific Risks: Regulations, currency restrictions, and political stability vary by country.
Buyer-Seller Relationship: Trust levels influence payment choice.
Competitive Landscape: Offering attractive payment terms (for importers) could be a differentiator.

Sources (Remember to cross-check and update)

Methods of Payment (US Trade Govt):
https://www.trade.gov/)
International Payments (Stripe):
https://stripe.com/resources/more/how-to-accept-
international-payments

The Not-So-Hidden Cost of Global Business

International transactions are thrilling for businesses –
new markets, fresh supply chains, exciting possibilities.
Yet, lurking beneath the surface is the often-overlooked
cost of foreign exchange (FX or forex). Every time you
pay an overseas supplier or get paid by a foreign client,
you're navigating the murky waters of currency
conversion.

Choosing the right FX provider is like having a skilled
boatman to guide you through these waters. A bad one
can leave you with unexpected fees and unfavorable
exchange rates that erode your profits.

Beyond the Big Banks: Demystifying FX Providers

Traditional Banks: The familiar option, but often come
with high fees and less-than-ideal exchange rates. Think
of them as the lumbering cruise ship of the FX world –
reliable, but not always the most efficient.
Specialist FX Brokers: These providers are the
speedboats of currency exchange. They focus solely on
FX, offering competitive rates and often, expert guidance
on market trends.
Online Marketplaces: These platforms act as
matchmakers, connecting businesses with a pool of FX

providers. Transparency is their superpower, allowing you to compare rates and fees easily.

The Search: Key Factors to Consider

Finding the right FX provider isn't just about the lowest rate. Consider these elements:

Exchange Rates: Obviously a priority. However, don't be fooled by a single number. Look at the spread (the difference between the "buy" and "sell" rate). A tighter spread means more of your money goes where it needs to.

Fees: The devil is in the details. Scrutinize transfer fees, markups, and any hidden charges.

Transfer Speed: Time is money. How fast does money move with a provider? Critical if you're facing tight payment deadlines.

Customer Support: When things inevitably get a little bumpy, you need someone in your corner. Look for responsive support with knowledgeable staff.

Hedging Tools: If you're dealing with large or frequent transactions, hedging tools can help manage currency risk and protect your bottom line.

Case Study: The Hidden Cost of Convenience

Company A relies on its bank for FX transactions. They get a rate of 1 USD = 0.87 EUR. They need to pay an invoice of €10,000.

Transaction cost with bank: €10,000 / 0.87 = $11,494.25
Company B uses a specialist FX broker with a rate of 1 USD = 0.89 EUR.

Transaction cost with broker: €10,000 / 0.89 = $11,235.96

Result: Company B saves $258.29 by opting for a dedicated FX provider. Imagine those savings scaled over multiple transactions!

Pro Tips: Words of Wisdom from the Trade

Negotiate like a pro: FX rates are not set in stone. Bigger volumes or a long-term relationship can potentially get you better rates.

Think beyond spot rates: If you have predictable future payments, forward contracts can help lock in favorable rates today for tomorrow's transactions.

"Batching" is your friend: Consolidating smaller payments into a larger one can sometimes reduce overall fees.

Where to Dig Deeper

This is just the tip of the iceberg! Here are some places to continue your research:

FX comparison sites: Websites like FXcompared help with side-by-side comparisons. [invalid URL removed]

Financial news outlets: Stay updated on the ever-changing FX market trends.

Case studies and testimonials: See how businesses like yours have benefited from switching providers.

Important Note: Regulations and laws governing FX can vary between countries. Always consult with relevant experts to ensure your chosen provider operates in compliance with the jurisdictions you do business in.

Chapter 17: Currency Impact on International Travel

Understanding the Currency Impact

International travel offers unparalleled experiences, but handling foreign exchange (FX) can be a headache. The constant dance of currencies can make or break a meticulously planned budget. Understanding this dynamic is crucial for cost-effective trips.

The Basics

Exchange Rates: An exchange rate tells you how much of one currency you'll get for another. For example, if 1 USD = 1.30 CAD, you'll receive 1.30 Canadian dollars for each US dollar.

Fluctuations: Exchange rates aren't set in stone – they change constantly based on economic factors, political events, and market speculation.

Budget Impact: A strong home currency means more buying power abroad. Conversely, if your currency weakens, the same trip becomes more expensive.

Case Study 1: The Euro Trip That Got Cheaper

Imagine Sarah, an American who planned a European vacation in 2020. Her budget was based on an exchange rate of 1 USD = 0.90 EUR. But when the pandemic struck, the US dollar strengthened, and by the time she traveled in 2021, the rate was 1 USD = 1.15 EUR. This meant Sarah got more euros for her dollars, effectively lowering accommodation, food, and activity costs.

Case Study 2: The Yen Surprise

Tom, a British traveler, has always dreamt of visiting Japan. In 2022, the exchange rate was around 1 GBP = 150 JPY. He budgeted carefully, but in 2023, the yen weakened significantly, reaching 1 GBP = 200 JPY. Suddenly, his trip seemed much more expensive, forcing him to re-evaluate his plans.

Unusual Angles to Consider

"Hidden" FX Costs: Don't forget ATM withdrawal fees, credit card foreign transaction fees, and dynamic currency conversion (DCC) offered by some merchants, which often carry unfavorable rates.
Strategic Timing: If possible, consider traveling during your home currency's strong periods or visiting destinations where your currency has greater purchasing power.
Geopolitical Hedging: Pay attention to major events that might impact currencies. Elections, trade tensions, or economic announcements can cause sudden shifts.

Strategies for Savvy Budgeting

Regularly Monitor Exchange Rates: Use reliable websites like [XE.com] (https://xe.com) or [OANDA] ([invalid URL removed]) to track trends.
Consider Multi-Currency Accounts: These accounts allow you to hold funds in various currencies, letting you "lock in" favorable rates when available.
Look for "Fee-Free" Financial Products: Some banks and credit cards waive foreign transaction fees, saving you significant costs.
Local Currency FTW: When possible, withdraw local cash upon arrival for smaller purchases. ATMs often offer better rates than currency exchange bureaus.

Hedge with Contracts (Advanced): For major trips or volatile currencies, consider forward contracts. These lock in an exchange rate for a future date, protecting you from fluctuations.

Sources for Further Research

[The Impact of Exchange Rates on International Travel] ([invalid URL removed])
BBC Worklife: What to do when exchange rates turn against you: https://www.bbc.com/worklife/tags/money

Important Note: Always double-check real-time exchange rates and fees with your financial institutions.

Navigating the Currency Maze for Savvy Travelers

International travel involves a fascinating dance with currencies. Understanding the nuances of foreign exchange (FX) can be the difference between a budget-friendly adventure and a wallet-draining nightmare. Let's break down the main players in FX and uncover some less-obvious strategies to make your travel dollars go further.

The Usual Suspects

Airport Bureaus: The siren call of convenience, airport exchange bureaus often offer the worst rates with high fees. These are your "break glass in case of emergency" options, better for small amounts to get you started.

Banks: Your home bank is likely a more reliable option. Exchange rates might be better, especially for larger amounts. Check for any international transaction fees they may charge.

ATMs: Often provide decent exchange rates, though be mindful of fees both from the ATM operator and your bank. Always use ATMs associated with reputable banks in safe, well-lit areas.

Unusual Angles for the Savvy Traveler

Credit Cards with No Foreign Transaction Fees: Some credit cards are travel-friendly, waiving the usual foreign transaction fees (often around 3%). This can save a significant amount, especially if you primarily use your card.

Online Currency Exchange Services: Platforms like Wise (formerly Transferwise) and others specialize in FX. They tend to offer better rates than traditional players.

Great for pre-ordering currency for pickup or delivery to your home.

"Dynamic Currency Conversion" Trap: Merchants may offer to bill you in your home currency. This seems helpful but often includes hidden markups on the exchange rate. Always opt to pay in the local currency.

Numerical Case Study: Trip to Europe

Let's imagine a €1000 budget for a week in Paris:

Scenario 1: Airport Kiosk - You might receive $950 USD after fees and poor rates. Loss of roughly 5%.

Scenario 2: Bank Exchange - Better rates and lower fees might get you $1050 USD. A substantial improvement.

Scenario 3: Savvy Traveler - Using the right credit card and ATMs, you could potentially stretch it close to $1100 USD. That's an extra €100 to spend!

Factors that Fluctuate the FX Market

The FX market isn't a monolith. Rates change constantly due to:

Global Economic Events: Wars, recessions, trade agreements, etc., all cause currency values to shift.

Interest Rates: Countries with higher interest rates tend to attract more foreign investment, boosting their currency values.

Political Stability: Investors flock towards currencies of politically stable nations seen as safer havens.

Pro Tips for Navigating the Currency Maze

Plan Ahead: Don't leave FX as an afterthought. Do some research about your destination's currency and optimal exchange strategies.

Keep a Currency Converter App Handy: Track exchange rates on the go for better decision-making.

Consider a "Borderless" Bank Account: Some online banks offer multiple currency accounts, making international spending smoother.

Sources (Remember, you'll need to verify info and look for more recent data)

[XE Currency Converter] (https://www.xe.com/)

[Nomad Capitalist - Best Ways to Exchange Currency] ([invalid URL removed])

Investopedia - Factors Affecting Exchange Rates: https://www.investopedia.com/terms/e/exchangerate.as p

This is just the beginning! Let's go further with:

Country-specific case studies (Japan's cash-centric culture vs. Sweden's use of cards)

Exploration of digital currencies and their potential for travel

Ethical considerations of haggling over exchange rates in developing countries.

Best Credit Cards for International Travel (Low Foreign Transaction Fees)

Foreign transaction fees can be a sneaky way for credit card issuers to squeeze extra money out of travelers. These fees, usually around 3% of each international purchase, can quickly add up. Choosing a card tailored for international use is a smart move for anyone planning a trip abroad.

Here are a few top picks to consider:

Chase Sapphire Preferred® Card: This versatile card offers solid rewards, welcome bonuses, and no foreign transaction fees. It's a popular choice for frequent travelers.

Capital One Venture X Rewards Credit Card: Looking for premium perks? This card may be an excellent fit, though a higher annual fee is involved. [https://www.capitalone.com/credit-cards/venture-x/]

Wells Fargo Autograph℠ Card: This no-annual-fee option still waives those pesky foreign transaction fees, making it a strong budget-friendly contender.

Important: Even with a great travel card, how you exchange currency still significantly impacts your spending power overseas.

Currency Impact on International Travel

Foreign exchange (forex) rates tell you how much of one currency you'll get for another. Unfortunately, this value fluctuates constantly! A seemingly small change can mean the difference between staying on budget and breaking the bank.

Case Study:

Let's say you're sipping a cappuccino in Rome. It costs €4, and today's USD/EUR exchange rate is 1.06. Here's how this can play out:

Scenario 1: Typical credit card: Your bank charges 3% for the foreign transaction, plus uses a less-than-ideal exchange rate (let's say 1.03). You end up paying around $4.05 in USD.

Scenario 2: Specialized travel card: No foreign transaction fee, and the card network (like Visa or Mastercard) offers a more competitive rate, closer to that 1.06. Your final price would be closer to $3.89 USD.

That might not seem like much, but scale it up over an entire trip, and those savings become significant!

Unusual Factors Impacting Forex:

Geopolitical Events: Wars, elections, and major policy changes can send ripples through forex markets.

Economic indicators: Things like a country's inflation rate, unemployment level, and trade balance influence the perceived strength of its currency.

Central Bank Intervention: Sometimes, central banks take direct action to stabilize or manipulate their currency's value.

How to Protect Yourself from Forex Headaches

Timing Matters: If possible, exchange some currency when rates are favorable rather than scrambling at the airport.

Avoid Tourist Traps: Airport kiosks and hotel currency exchanges usually offer the worst rates.

Consider specialist providers: Services like Wise (https://wise.com/) often beat bank rates for larger transfers.

Hedge (if you're fancy): For very large transactions or extended trips, advanced hedging strategies might be worth exploring, although these tend to be more the territory of businesses than casual travelers.

Unusual Word Choices

To help avoid sounding overly generic, consider sprinkling in phrases like:

"Choosing the right card is like having a currency converter in your wallet."
"Don't let unfavorable exchange rates leave a sour taste in your mouth."

Remember: Credit card offers, exchange rates, and even global events can change rapidly. It's vital to do your own up-to-date research tailored to your specific destinations and travel dates.

Strategies for Timing Currency Conversions

Currency exchange, or foreign exchange (forex), is a constant dance for the international traveler. Converting your home currency at the "right" time can mean the difference between a budget-friendly dream trip or a wallet-busting experience.

The Basics: Why Exchange Rates Matter

Purchasing Power: When your home currency is strong relative to your destination's, your money stretches further. Think of it like a superpower – your dollars, euros, or pounds suddenly buy more local goods and services.

Hidden Fees: Exchange bureaus, banks, and ATMs often have hidden fees on top of the stated exchange rate. Understanding these helps you avoid unpleasant surprises.

Standard Timing Strategies

Gradual Conversion: Instead of converting all your money at once, spread transactions over time. This averages out your exchange rate, reducing risk from sudden swings.

Set Rate Alerts: Services like Google Finance can alert you when your target exchange rate is reached, helping time your conversion for optimal value.

Pre-Trip Purchases: For significant expenses (tours, hotels), sometimes pre-booking and paying in the destination currency can lock in a favorable rate, offering predictability.

Unusual Tactics: Beyond the Basics

"News Hound" Approach: Big economic or political events can trigger currency fluctuations. Keep an eye on your destination's news cycle and try to exchange when their currency is temporarily weaker.

Exploit the "Carry Trade": This advanced strategy involves borrowing in a country with low interest rates and converting to a currency offering higher rates. Word of Caution: Carry trades are high-risk, suitable for experienced traders only.

The Nomad Strategy: If your travel is flexible, consider basing yourself temporarily in a country with a favorable exchange rate relative to your desired destinations. Live cheaply, explore widely!

Numerical Case Studies

USD to EUR (2023): A traveler converting $1000 USD in January might get ~930 EUR. But waiting until July, that same $1000 could be worth ~1050 EUR – a significant difference! (Source: https://www.xe.com/currencycharts/?from=USD&to=EUR&view=1Y)

The Brexit Effect (2016): The UK's vote to leave the EU caused the pound sterling (GBP) to plummet. A £50 hotel room pre-Brexit was much steeper once the pound weakened. (Source: BBC - Brexit and the Pound)

Advanced AI Tools

Predictive Analytics: Some services utilize AI algorithms to analyze historical data and forecast short-term exchange trends. Use with caution, as currency markets are notoriously unpredictable.

Sentiment Analysis: AI can scan news and social media to assess the "mood" around a currency. A sudden spike in negative sentiment might signal a potential weakening.

Important Reminders

There is no crystal ball: Forex is complex. Even the best strategies can be caught out by unexpected events.

Diversify your approach: Combine different timing techniques, and keep some cash in your home currency for emergencies.

"Perfect" is the enemy of "good enough": Over-analyzing can lead to missed opportunities. Sometimes, a decent exchange rate today is better than chasing the elusive "perfect" one.

Avoiding Common Travel Currency Scams

International travel is exhilarating, but navigating foreign exchange (FX) can be a minefield of scams and hidden fees. Tourists are prime targets: they're often unfamiliar with local currency and may be in a hurry. A little knowledge goes a long way in protecting your hard-earned travel budget.

Types of Scams

Shortchanging: Cashiers, especially in busy areas, might 'accidentally' give you incorrect change, hoping you won't notice. Always count your money carefully.

The 'Helpful' Local: Someone offers to calculate exchange rates for you, using rates wildly in their favor, pocketing the difference.

Fake Currency: Older notes may be out of circulation or counterfeit bills passed off, especially in low-light situations. Look for security features, or feel the unique texture of official notes.

Dynamic Currency Conversion (DCC): ATMs or merchants might ask if you want to be charged in your home currency. This seems convenient, but hides terrible exchange rates. Decline and always pay in the local currency.

Case Study: The Taxi "Special Rate"

You hail a taxi at the airport, excited to reach your hotel. The driver offers a "special fixed rate" in your home currency. It sounds fair, but later you realize you paid double the standard metered fare.

Numerical Impact

Imagine a $50 USD taxi ride converted at a scammer's rate of 1 USD = 0.80 Euros, instead of the official rate of around 1 USD = 0.95 Euros. You unknowingly overpaid by roughly 10 Euros! Small amounts add up over a trip.

Protection Strategies

Pre-Trip Preparation:
Research official exchange rates before you leave ([XE.com] (https://xe.com) is a reliable source)
Get small bills in the local currency at your home bank for initial expenses.
Use Official Exchange Bureaus: Generally offer the best rates. Compare a few, and avoid those in heavily touristed areas which may have higher fees.
Credit Cards: Many have no foreign transaction fees, letting you tap into the fair interbank exchange rate. However, notify your bank about travel plans to avoid fraud blocks.

Mobile Apps: Currency conversion apps help calculate costs on the spot.

Be Vigilant:

Have a calculator handy to double-check rates offered on the fly.

If something feels off, politely decline. It's okay to walk away.

Unusual Angle: The 'Broken Calculator' Scam

Less common, but worth noting: A shopkeeper offers to calculate an exchange, their calculator conveniently shows an outrageous rate. They claim it's broken, aiming to confuse you into overpaying.

Maximizing Your Travel Budget

Bargaining Power: Paying in local currency can offer leverage when haggling in markets (if appropriate to the local culture).

Cashback Options: Some credit cards offer cashback on international purchases, slightly offsetting fees.

The ATM Factor: While convenient, ATMs often charge fees. If you must use one, withdraw larger amounts less frequently to minimize overall fees.

Remember: A bit of research and awareness can significantly reduce your risk of falling prey to currency scams. Protecting your finances allows you to focus on what matters most – experiencing the joys of travel.

Chapter 18: Investing in a Global Market

Benefits of Portfolio Diversification with Foreign Assets

In the age of interwoven economies, diversifying your portfolio with foreign assets is no longer a luxury – it's a financial imperative. Let's dive into the advantages, strategies, and some number-crunching that illustrates just how savvy foreign asset allocation can be.

Why Bother With Foreign Assets?

Breaking Free from Domestic Limitations: Your home market can only offer so much. Foreign assets offer exposure to different industries, growth trajectories, and economic cycles that you can't find at home.

The Currency Hedge: When your domestic currency wobbles, foreign assets denominated in stronger currencies can cushion the blow. Think of them as 'financial lifeboats' during choppy market waters.

Chasing Growth Opportunities: Many emerging markets boast significantly higher growth rates compared to developed ones. Foreign assets let you tap into that dynamism.

Case Study: The Resilient Portfolio

Let's imagine two investors, Sarah and Ben:

Sarah builds a portfolio of only domestic stocks, primarily from the tech sector.

Ben has a similar allocation but diversifies with 30% foreign assets, including emerging market stocks and bonds.

A domestic tech slump hits. Sarah's portfolio takes a significant hit. Meanwhile, Ben's foreign holdings perform well in other economies, mitigating the overall losses to his portfolio.

The Art of Smart Diversification

Simply buying any foreign asset won't do. Here's what to keep in mind:

Developed vs. Emerging Markets: Developed markets offer stability, while emerging ones provide the potential for higher (but riskier) returns. Find a balance that matches your risk tolerance.
Correlation is Key: The true magic of diversification lies in assets that don't move in sync. Look for investments that have a low or negative correlation to your existing holdings.
Currency Risk: Exchange rates fluctuate, adding another layer of complexity (and potential gain) to foreign assets. Consider hedging strategies if you're concerned about significant currency swings.

Unusual Angles to Consider

"Thematic" Foreign Investing: Instead of just countries, think in themes. ETFs focused on renewable energy, for example, give you international exposure centered on a specific sector.
Geopolitical Hedging: Including assets from politically stable regions can protect your portfolio if your home country faces economic or political turmoil.

Tools of the Trade

Foreign ETFs/Mutual Funds: The easiest way to gain broad foreign exposure. [Source: Investopedia: Foreign ETFs]
Individual Foreign Stocks: Requires more research, but offers greater control.
Foreign Bonds: Provide income and can have low correlation to stocks. [Source: Vanguard – Investing in Foreign Bonds]

Important Note: Foreign assets introduce unique risk factors. Do your due diligence regarding taxation, regulatory differences, and market access before investing.

Final Thoughts

Building a globally diversified portfolio is a journey of constant learning and adaptation. Done right, it's like giving your investments a set of superpowers to weather market storms and capitalize on worldwide opportunities.

Exploring Direct Investment vs. ADRs for Global Exposure

The world of investing isn't confined by borders. Expanding a portfolio internationally offers diversification and the potential to tap into the growth of foreign markets. But how does one gain that overseas exposure? There are two primary routes:

Direct Investment in Foreign Stocks: This is the purest, most unfiltered form of foreign investment. You purchase shares of a foreign company directly on its home exchange.

American Depository Receipts (ADRs): These are certificates issued by a U.S. bank representing shares of a foreign company. ADRs trade on U.S. exchanges, streamlining the process for American investors.

The Case for Direct Investment

Granular Control: Direct investment grants you complete control over the specific companies you invest in. It's great for investors seeking niche opportunities that ADRs might not cover.
Potential Cost Savings: In some cases, avoiding the middleman of an ADR can mean lower transaction fees.
Authenticity: Some investors relish the feeling of owning a piece of a company directly on its home market.

Challenges of Direct Investment

Navigational Complexities: Each foreign market operates with its own rules, regulations, and often a language barrier. This can be a complex landscape for a U.S. investor.

Currency Risk: Your returns are affected not only by the stock's performance but by shifts in the exchange rate between the foreign currency and the U.S. dollar.
Liquidity: Some foreign markets, especially in emerging regions, may have lower trading volumes, making it harder to buy or sell shares quickly.

The Appeal of ADRs

Convenience: ADRs trade in U.S. dollars on U.S. exchanges during standard market hours. This familiarity streamlines the whole process.
Accessibility of Information: Companies issuing ADRs often translate their financial reports into English and comply with U.S. disclosure standards, making research easier.
Reduced Currency Risk: Though foreign exchange still plays a role, the bank issuing an ADR generally handles currency translations.

The Caveats of ADRs

Fees: ADRs often involve additional fees from the issuing bank, potentially eating into returns.
Limited Selection: Not every foreign company has an ADR program, limiting your choices.
Voting Rights: ADRs sometimes involve varying degrees of ownership rights compared to holding the foreign shares directly.

Numerical Case Study: ADR vs. Direct

Let's imagine investing $10,000 in a hot German tech stock called "Blitz AG."

Direct Investment: Your $10,000 is converted to euros at the exchange rate. You buy shares on the Frankfurt

exchange, paying brokerage fees in euros. Blitz AG's share price AND fluctuations between the euro and dollar influence your gains/losses.
ADR: You find Blitz AG's ADR listed on the NYSE. You purchase shares in dollars with standard U.S. brokerage fees. Blitz AG's price, the issuing bank's fees, AND the dollar/euro exchange rate affect your investment.

Unusual Angles to Consider

Tax Headaches: Foreign tax laws, the potential for double taxation, and differing tax treatment of ADRs add a layer of complexity. Consulting a tax professional may be wise.
Geopolitical Risk: Investing across borders injects geopolitical uncertainty into the equation. Trade disputes, sanctions, or regional conflicts can rock even well-established foreign companies.

Sources

[Investopedia on ADRs]
(https://www.investopedia.com/terms/a/adr.asp)
[Schwab International on Investing in Foreign Stocks]
(https://international.schwab.com/investment-products/adrs-foreign-ordinaries-canadian-stocks)

Currency Considerations when Investing in Foreign Bonds

Investing in foreign bonds provides diversification benefits, but also introduces an often-overlooked factor: currency risk. Unlike domestic bonds where returns are in your home currency, foreign bonds carry the added uncertainty of exchange rate fluctuations.

The Mechanics of Currency Impact

Let's break down how currency movements affect foreign bond returns:

Scenario 1: Foreign Currency Strengthens
Imagine buying a Japanese bond denominated in yen, with a 5% yield. If the yen strengthens against your home currency (say, the US dollar) by 3% during your holding period, your overall return jumps. The 5% yield, converted back to dollars, yields an effective return of approximately 8%.

Scenario 2: Foreign Currency Weakens
The opposite is also true. If the yen weakens by 3% against the dollar, that 5% bond yield suddenly translates into a meager 2% return in dollar terms.

Case Study: The Euro's Impact

Let's consider a historical example. An American investor purchases a German bond in 2010, denominated in euros. Over the next few years, the euro strengthens against the dollar. Even if the bond itself offers a modest yield, the investor's overall return is boosted significantly by the favorable exchange rate movement. Conversely, the eurozone crisis later causes the euro to weaken – a negative headwind for the investor's overall returns.

Unexpected Angles & Nuances

The standard advice is to hedge currency risk or buy bonds denominated in your home currency. But, there are some less-discussed subtleties:

Inflation Hedges: Sometimes, currency depreciation in the bond's country of origin might correlate with higher inflation there. The bond's underlying returns might partially offset the negative impact of currency depreciation, offering a peculiar inflation hedge.

Tactical Currency Views: Active investors may deliberately bet on currency movements. If you have a strong belief that a particular currency will appreciate, buying bonds denominated in that currency adds a "leveraged" dimension to your speculative position. (Naturally, this involves higher risk).

"Carry Trade" Considerations: Bonds in higher-yielding currencies often appear attractive. However, those currencies might be more prone to depreciation, partially or wholly offsetting the interest rate advantage.

Unusual Word Choices

To infuse your writing with unique phrasing, consider words like:

Conundrum: "The currency conundrum faced by foreign bond investors..."
Vicissitudes: "...the inherent vicissitudes of currency markets..."
Augment: "...currency movements can dramatically augment foreign bond returns..."

Advanced AI & Research

To go deeper, consider these resources and techniques:

Historical Currency Data: Analyze past exchange rate data for relevant currency pairs (e.g., USD/EUR, USD/JPY) to understand potential volatility. [XE.com] (https://xe.com) is a good starting point.
Real-World Market Analysis: Use financial news platforms like Bloomberg or Reuters to track current market commentary on currency movements and their expected impact on bond markets.
Economic Forecasts: Central bank websites and economic research institutions frequently publish forecasts for exchange rates. Understanding the factors driving those forecasts can inform your investment decisions.

Remember: Foreign bonds introduce a unique dimension to fixed income investing. Grasping the nuances of currency risk and the potential for both enhanced gains and unexpected losses will help you successfully navigate the global bond market.

Accessing Foreign Real Estate Markets: ETFs vs. Direct Investment

Investing in property outside your home country can open up exciting opportunities. But how do you go about it? The two main methods are exchange-traded funds (ETFs) and direct investment, each with its own pros and cons.

ETFs: The Simpler Route

What are they? ETFs are like baskets of stocks, in this case, real estate stocks from a particular foreign market. This lets you invest in a whole segment of a country's market in one go.
Pros: Easy to buy and sell, offer diversification, and tend to have lower management fees than actively managed funds
Cons: Less control over individual investments, and you're exposed to currency fluctuations between your home currency and that of the target market.

Direct Investment: Hands-On with Potential for Higher Rewards

What it means: Buying actual properties overseas, whether residential, commercial, or even raw land.
Pros: Potential for greater returns, direct control over your assets, and possible tax benefits depending on your home country and your investment location.
Cons: Requires significant research, due diligence, potential language barriers, and understanding of local regulations. Can be highly illiquid, meaning it may take a while to sell your property if needed.

Unusual Factors to Consider

Geopolitical stability: Is the country you're interested in facing turmoil? This can make property values volatile or leave you with unexpected legal hurdles.

"Boots on the ground": With direct investment, having a trusted local contact (realtor, lawyer, property manager) is crucial to help you navigate the market and handle ongoing issues.

Hidden costs: Property taxes, maintenance, legal fees, and even the cost of obtaining a visa if you plan to visit may surprise you when investing abroad.

Numerical Case Studies

Let's imagine you're a US-based investor with $100,000 to put towards foreign real estate:

Scenario 1: ETF
You invest in an ETF tracking the Japanese real estate market. Over 5 years, it sees a 6% annual growth rate, but the US dollar strengthens against the Yen by 5%. Your net return is closer to 1% per year.

Scenario 2: Direct Investment
You buy a condo in a developing coastal town in Portugal. The property appreciates by 12% annually for 5 years. However, legal fees, currency exchange expenses, and unforeseen repairs eat up 3% per year. Net return: around 9% annually.

The Verdict: It Depends

The "best" way to access foreign real estate depends heavily on the following:

Risk tolerance: Are you comfortable with a potentially more volatile direct investment?

Time horizon: ETFs can be good for shorter timeframes, while the potential rewards of direct investment might justify a longer-term commitment. Level of involvement: Do you want a mostly passive investment (ETFs) or are you ready to roll up your sleeves and manage properties yourself?

Finding Information and Avoiding AI "Sameness"

Look beyond generic financial sites for information to spice up your writing. Here are some ideas:

Country-specific real estate blogs: Local agents often share market insights
Government websites: Look for foreign investment regulations on official websites of the country you're interested in.
Case studies on lesser-known markets: [This article about Montenegro's property market offers an unusual angle] ([invalid URL removed])

Important Note: Investing always carries an element of risk, and this is especially true when dealing with unfamiliar markets. Thorough research and legal/financial advice are crucial before putting any money down.

Managing Tax Implications of Foreign Investments

Investing in a global market offers opportunities for diversification and growth, but it also introduces additional tax considerations beyond domestic investing. Understanding the intricacies of foreign taxation is crucial to maximizing your returns and avoiding nasty surprises.

Key Areas of Tax Impact

Double Taxation: A major pain point! Many countries tax income earned within their borders, regardless of the investor's residency. This means you could get taxed twice on the same income – once by the country where the investment originates, and again by your home country.

Foreign Tax Credits: Often designed to mitigate double taxation, these credits allow you to offset taxes paid to foreign governments against your domestic tax liability. However, the rules and limitations around these credits can be complex.

Withholding Taxes: Many countries impose withholding taxes on dividends and interest payments made to foreign investors. These taxes are deducted at the source, reducing the income you actually receive.

Currency Exchange Fluctuations: When you invest in foreign assets, your returns are affected by changes in exchange rates between your home currency and the currency of the investment. Currency gains or losses can have tax implications.

Case Study: The Impact of Withholding Taxes

Let's say you're a US investor who purchased shares in a German company that pays a dividend of €100. Germany has a 25% dividend withholding tax rate. Here's the potential impact:

Gross Dividend: €100
Withholding tax (25%): €25
Net Dividend Received: €75

Additionally, you would need to convert the €75 back to US dollars, adding the element of currency exchange rates.

Navigating the Complexities

Tax Treaties: Many countries have tax treaties with each other that aim to reduce or eliminate double taxation and lower withholding tax rates. Familiarize yourself with the treaties relevant to your investments.

Tax Efficient Investment Vehicles: Certain structures like foreign investment funds or exchange-traded funds (ETFs) may offer tax advantages, depending on your circumstances.

Foreign Income Exclusion (US-Specific): US taxpayers may be able to exclude a certain amount of foreign earned income from their taxable income. However, limitations and qualifications apply.

Unusual Considerations

Passive Foreign Investment Companies (PFICs): Investing in certain foreign companies classified as PFICs by the IRS can trigger complex and punitive tax rules (US-specific).

Controlled Foreign Corporations (CFCs): If you own a significant stake in a foreign corporation, special tax rules may apply (US-specific).

FATCA (Foreign Account Tax Compliance Act): US citizens and residents may need to report their foreign financial accounts, including foreign investments.

Case Study: The Hidden Costs of PFICs

Consider a US investor who unknowingly invests in a mutual fund classified as a PFIC. They don't immediately sell their shares, so the gains accumulate within the fund. Later, when they do sell, they could face:

Higher income tax rates on the gains
Interest charges on the deferred taxes
Complex reporting requirements

Sources:

IRS Publication 514 - Foreign Tax Credit: https://www.irs.gov/individuals/international-taxpayers/foreign-tax-credit)
Investopedia - Understanding Taxation of Foreign Investments: https://www.investopedia.com/terms/f/foreign-investment.asp
The Impact of FATCA: https://www.investopedia.com/terms/f/foreign-account-tax-compliance-act-fatca.asp

Section VI: Advanced Topics

Chapter 19: Algorithmic and High-Frequency Trading

Understanding Algorithmic Trading

Algorithmic trading is like giving your FX trading strategy a robot assistant. It uses pre-programmed rules and calculations to make lightning-fast decisions about buying and selling currencies. High-frequency trading (HFT) is a super-charged version of algorithmic trading, focused on milliseconds-long trades for tiny profits that add up over many trades.

Let's delve into a few popular algorithmic trading strategies, offering some unusual twists for that standout factor you're after:

1. Arbitrage: Spotting Tiny Mispricings

The Basic Idea: Arbitrageurs are the eagle-eyed detectives of the market. They pounce on situations where the same currency pair has slightly different prices on different exchanges. They buy low, sell high – pocketing the difference.
Unusual Angle: In FX, the speed of arbitrage is crazy important. Ever heard of triangular arbitrage? It's where you swap currencies across three exchanges to exploit price differences. Takes serious tech and lightning-fast reflexes!
Case Study (Hypothetical): Let's say EUR/USD is trading at 1.0500 on Exchange A, but 1.0502 on Exchange B. An arbitrageur with razor-sharp algorithms might buy EUR 1,000,000 on Exchange A and

immediately sell it on Exchange B, netting a profit of $200 before fees. Doesn't sound like much, but scale that across thousands of trades a day...
Source: [Investopedia on Triangular Arbitrage] (https://www.investopedia.com/terms/t/triangulararbitr age.asp)

2. Trend-Following: Riding the Currency Waves

The Basic Idea: Trend-followers are like surfers, trying to catch the momentum of an exchange rate. They use things like moving averages or technical indicators to figure out if a currency is trending up, down, or sideways
Unusual Angle: Combining trend-following with unusual indicators can spice things up. Maybe look at on-balance volume (OBV) to analyze how buying and selling pressure might be influencing a trend change in the FX market.
Case Study (Simplified): Imagine EUR/USD has been steadily rising for a week. Its 50-day moving average crosses above the 100-day moving average (a bullish signal). A trend-following algo, looking at both price and OBV, might take a long position, hoping to ride the uptrend.
Source: [Technical Indicators in Forex] ([invalid URL removed])

3. News-Based Trading: Robots Reading Headlines

The Basic Idea: These algorithms are news junkies. They use natural language processing (NLP) to scan headlines, social media, you name it – seeking info that might move exchange rates. Did the Fed Chair say something surprising? Algorithms can react in milliseconds.
Unusual Angle: News-based trading isn't just about the big stuff. Maybe track sentiment across regional news

249

sources. Are central banks hinting at policy shifts? Or maybe news about commodity prices could give clues about currency movements.

Case Study (Hypothetical): An algorithm with NLP capability detects news of a sudden decline in oil futures. Historically, this has correlated with a weakening of the Canadian Dollar. The algorithm might trigger a short trade on CAD/USD to potentially exploit this relationship.

Source: [The Challenges of Sentiment Analysis] ([invalid URL removed])

Important Considerations and Caveats

The Arms Race: Algo trading is constantly evolving. The most successful traders keep their strategies super secret, creating a whole world of 'black box' trading.

Beyond the Basics: There are TONS more algorithms out there – statistical arbitrage, mean reversion, the whole wide world of machine learning. This is just a taste!

Liquidity Risks: Especially in HFT, filling your orders at the right price is crucial. Huge trades can move the market before your algo has a chance to fully execute.

Tech Matters: Algo trading needs serious computer power, rock-solid coding, and crazy fast market data access. This isn't for the casual trader.

High-Frequency Trading Strategies & Techniques

Algorithmic and high-frequency trading (HFT) have revolutionized global financial markets, and the foreign exchange market is no exception. HFT's emphasis on lightning-fast execution, complex algorithms, and the processing of massive data sets makes it particularly well-suited for the fast-paced, highly liquid world of FX.

Let's dive into some strategies and techniques used in FX HFT, but we'll intentionally look at them from less common angles to spark your further research:

1. Statistical Arbitrage: Beyond the Basics

Stat arb, as it's often called, seeks to exploit fleeting price discrepancies between correlated assets. Here's where it gets interesting:

Triangular Arbitrage, Twisted: Instead of focusing on classic currency triads (e.g., EUR/USD, USD/JPY, EUR/JPY), HFT might find success in far more obscure cross-currency correlations. Think emerging market currencies or complex currency derivatives.
The "Whisper" of Correlations: HFT algorithms might uncover transient correlations based not just on price but on volatility patterns, unexpected news impacts, or even subtle shifts in order flow.

2. "Sniping" Liquidity: The Art of the Stealthy Order

Liquidity provision is a delicate game. HFT firms often provide it, but sometimes, they hunt for it with these unusual tactics:
The Ghost in the Machine: Instead of posting visible limit orders, algorithms might use hidden order types, or

fleetingly place and cancel orders to probe market depth without tipping their hand.

Predatory Icebergs: Large orders split into tiny slices and dispersed over time ("iceberg" orders) are common, but HFT could take it further. Imagine algorithms that randomly vary the size, timing, and even the exchange for their iceberg slices to throw off their competitors.

3. News Algorithms: When Sentiment is Data

News-based HFT is well-known, but let's look at the less conventional side:

Beyond the Headlines: While most algorithms focus on big macroeconomic announcements, HFT might specialize in niche data points – regional economic figures, central bank speeches, even weather reports with potential FX impact.

The Language of the Market: Natural language processing (NLP) can help algorithms interpret sentiment, but what about the tone of news articles, social media sentiment, or even shifts in geopolitical language?

Case Studies (Hypothetical – To Encourage Your Own Research)

The Emerging Market Blitz: An HFT algorithm detects a momentary correlation spike between the Mexican Peso and the Chilean Peso due to similar copper export exposure. It executes a rapid cross-currency arbitrage trade, profiting from the temporary mispricing.

Order Book Illusion: An HFT firm wants to buy a large EUR/USD block. Its algorithm floods the order book with tiny sell orders slightly above the market price, tricking other algorithms into thinking there's downward pressure and pushing them to lower their bids.

Important Considerations and Caveats

Regulation: The Evolving Landscape HFT regulation is complex and region-specific. Research the latest rules in your target jurisdictions to avoid compliance issues. [Source example: ESMA's work on algorithmic trading] The Speed Demon's Achilles Heel: Infrastructure is king. Co-location, fiber-optic cables, and even custom hardware matter just as much as the algorithm when nanoseconds count. Investigate the technology arms race. Market Impact: The Ghost That Moves the Price HFT strategies can accidentally shift prices against themselves, especially in less liquid currency pairs or during volatile events.

HFT and FX Liquidity

Introduction

High-frequency trading (HFT) has transformed financial markets, and the foreign exchange market is no exception. Powered by sophisticated algorithms and lightning-fast execution speeds, HFT firms capitalize on minute price discrepancies and fleeting market trends. The question remains: does this relentless pursuit of micro-opportunities ultimately benefit or harm overall market liquidity?

What is Liquidity (in the FX Context)?

In simple terms, FX market liquidity refers to the ease with which you can buy or sell currencies without causing significant price swings. Imagine a market with deep liquidity – you can trade large amounts without drastically impacting the exchange rate. Conversely, in a market with thin liquidity, even modest transactions can cause substantial price shifts.

HFT: The Liquidity Providers

Adding Depth to the Order Book: HFT algorithms constantly place and update bids and offers at various price levels, adding depth to order books. This means potential buyers and sellers have more options, making transactions smoother.

Tightening Bid-Ask Spreads: The bid-ask spread is the difference between buying and selling prices. HFT competition compels market makers to narrow those spreads, lowering transaction costs for all participants.

Speed Advantage: HFT can react with incredible speed to news events or market shifts, quickly updating quotes to reflect new information. This efficiency helps prices adjust faster, reducing the time it takes for the market to find a new equilibrium.

HFT: Potential Liquidity Drainers

Phantom Liquidity: Critics argue HFT liquidity is illusory. Algorithms can flood the order book with bids and offers that vanish within milliseconds, making true market depth difficult to gauge.

Flash Crashes and Volatility: While debatable, some studies suggest HFT strategies can exacerbate sudden price swings or "flash crashes." Algorithms acting in unison may unintentionally amplify market turbulence during periods of stress.

Preying on Slower Traders: HFT can profit by detecting and exploiting the orders of slower market participants (e.g., institutional investors). This "picking off" behavior can increase implicit trading costs for those with less technological muscle.

Numerical Case Studies (Illustrative – Need Real Data)

Example 1: Compare bid-ask spreads on a major currency pair (e.g., EUR/USD) before and after a surge in HFT activity in that market. Does the spread consistently narrow?

Example 2: Track market depth during a news event. Do HFT firms provide consistent liquidity through the volatility, or do large orders start to "chew through" the order book more quickly?

Example 3: During a suspected period of predatory HFT, examine order submission and cancellation patterns. Is there evidence that large orders are placed, smaller traders react, and then the large order is withdrawn?

Unusual Angles to Consider

Ecosystem Impact: HFT creates winners and losers. Could its effects on liquidity indirectly hinder long-term investment strategies that rely on stable markets?

Arms Race: Constant technological innovation is the name of the game. This relentless pursuit may impose high costs on smaller firms and contribute to a "winner-takes-all" market structure.

Latency Arbitrage: Some HFT profits derive from exploiting minute speed differences between trading venues. This activity may provide little fundamental value to the market as a whole.

Sources (Starting Points)

[Does high-frequency trading actually improve market liquidity? A comparative study for selected models and measures] (https://ideas.repec.org/a/eee/riibaf/v64y2023ics027553 1922002586.html)

Corporate Finance Institute on HFT:
https://corporatefinanceinstitute.com/resources/equities
/high-frequency-trading-hft/
Algorithmic and High-Frequency Trading | Market
Liquidity - Oxford Academic:
https://academic.oup.com/book/55158/chapter/424085
051

Algorithmic Trading in FX

Algorithmic trading, the practice of letting code execute your trades, has upended financial markets. The foreign exchange market (FX), with its colossal volume and 24/7 operation, provides a particularly fertile ground for algorithmic strategies. In this piece, we'll delve into the nuts and bolts of building FX trading systems, the languages that make them tick, and the art of backtesting.

The FX Advantage (and Why Algos Love It)

Liquidity Redefined: FX is the world's most liquid market, with trillions of dollars changing hands daily. This liquidity means algorithms can usually find willing buyers or sellers, a crucial factor for minimizing slippage (the difference between your targeted price and where the trade actually executes).

Around the Clock: FX trades 24 hours a day (with slight pauses on weekends). This continuous operation gives algorithms more chances to find potential signals and execute across different timeframes.

It's All Relative: FX revolves around trading currency pairs (e.g., EUR/USD). This focus on relative values creates opportunities for statistical and arbitrage-based strategies.

Programming Languages: The Tools of the Algo Trade

The Python Powerhouse: Python's dominance is undeniable. Its clarity, massive libraries (NumPy, Pandas, scikit-learn), and dedicated algo-trading communities solidify its position. It's the go-to choice for many, especially those who are newer to coding.

C++: When Speed is of the Essence: For the ultimate in raw performance and low-level control, C++ is king. Frequently seen in high-frequency trading (HFT), where microseconds matter, C++ requires greater programming expertise to harness its power.

The Versatility of Java: Java's a solid contender, especially for established systems. Its strength lies in building robust, large-scale platforms. Less widespread than Python in FX-specific algo trading, it remains a viable option.

R: The Statistician's Friend: While not as common for building live trading systems, R excels at statistical analysis and modeling. Its capabilities are valuable for research and backtesting potential strategies.

Backtesting: Turning the Clock Back (Responsibly)

Backtesting is the simulated trading of your strategy using historical data. It's a sanity check, not a crystal ball. Here's why a healthy dose of skepticism is vital:

The Overfitting Peril: It's easy to craft a system that perfectly fits past data. But will it work in the unpredictable future? Robust backtesting means striking a delicate balance between tailoring your strategy to historical patterns and avoiding the trap of chasing ghosts in the data.

Data: Not All Is Created Equal: The quality and source of your data matter immensely. Using inaccurate or heavily filtered data can skew your results, giving a false sense of security.

Case Studies (with a Pinch of Salt)

Trend Following on the Majors: A classic algo strategy might look for sustained moves in major pairs (EUR/USD, GBP/USD, etc.). Indicators like moving averages can help identify trends, with rules for trade entry and exit.

The Arbitrage Angle: Short-lived discrepancies occasionally emerge between the same currency pair on different exchanges. Algorithms can be designed to swoop in and exploit these tiny price differences through high-speed trades.

News-Based Sentiment: This higher-risk area involves building systems that attempt to parse news events, gauge market sentiment (positive/negative), and trade accordingly.

Important Considerations (and a Reality Check)

The Edge Isn't Easy: Retail traders face stiff competition. Banks, hedge funds, and HFT firms invest heavily in algo development. Sustainable strategies often require a blend of financial knowledge, coding skill, and continuous research.

Infrastructure Matters: Especially for HFT, low-latency connectivity, proximity to exchanges, and powerful hardware become crucial ingredients.

Don't Forget the Human: Algo trading shouldn't be completely "set and forget". It requires oversight, risk parameters, and the ability to intervene when needed.

Risks and Controversies of Algorithmic Trading

While algorithmic and high-frequency trading (HFT) offer speed and automation to trading, these technologies also bring a unique set of risks and controversies into the foreign exchange (FX) market. Understanding these pitfalls is crucial as algorithmic dominance in the FX space continues to grow.

1. The Illusion of Control and Over-Reliance

The Paradox of Automation: It's tempting to think that the precise, calculated nature of algorithmic trading eliminates human error. However, algorithms are only as good as their programming and the data they're trained on. Unexpected market shifts or "black swan" events can lead to catastrophic losses if algorithms aren't equipped to handle them.

"Algo Arms Race": As algorithmic trading becomes more prevalent, firms race to develop faster, more sophisticated systems. This can lead to over-optimization on historical data and a lack of adaptability to changing market conditions.

2. Exacerbated Volatility and Flash Crashes

Herding Behavior: HFT algorithms, especially those using similar strategies, can inadvertently amplify market movements. When a large number of algorithms react to the same signal, they can trigger cascading buy or sell orders, leading to exaggerated price swings and even temporary market collapses.

The May 6, 2010 Flash Crash: This event saw the Dow Jones Industrial Average plunge by nearly 1000 points in minutes. While not solely attributable to HFT, it highlighted how interconnected markets and algorithmic trading can increase systemic fragility.

3. Liquidity: A Double-Edged Sword

The Liquidity Mirage: HFT firms often provide liquidity by placing numerous small orders that can be quickly withdrawn. This paints a picture of a robust market, but that liquidity can vanish instantly under stress conditions, potentially leaving other traders stranded. Liquidity Fragmentation: Algorithms can route orders to less transparent venues like dark pools, potentially making it harder to get a true picture of market depth and price discovery.

4. Ethical Quandaries and Market Manipulation

Front-Running: Due to their speed, HFT firms may have an informational advantage, placing their orders ahead of larger ones detected in the market. This can create an unfair advantage and potentially erode confidence in market fairness.
Spoofing and Layering: Algorithms can be used to place large orders they intend to cancel, tricking others into trading in a certain direction. These manipulative tactics are detrimental to legitimate traders.

5. Technological Barrier to Entry

The Cost of Speed: Developing and maintaining HFT systems requires substantial investment in infrastructure and talent. This can create a competitive barrier that favors large institutions and may squeeze out smaller players.
The Black Box Problem: The complexity of algorithmic trading strategies can make it hard to understand their behavior in all market scenarios. This

creates oversight challenges for regulators and makes it harder for investors to fully assess risk.

Case Studies: When Algorithms Go Awry

Knight Capital Fiasco (2012): A software glitch caused Knight Capital to flood the market with errant orders, resulting in a $440 million loss in a mere 45 minutes. [[invalid URL removed]]
UBS Rogue Trader Incident (2011): A trader lost $2.3 billion using unauthorized algorithms to hide his positions. It highlights the risk of unchecked algorithms and poor internal controls. [[invalid URL removed]]

Mitigating Risks: A Work in Progress

Regulators globally are grappling with the challenges posed by algorithmic trading. Measures being explored include:

"Circuit Breakers": Pauses in trading during extreme volatility.
Minimum Resting Times: Requiring orders to remain active for a brief period to discourage fleeting bids/offers.
Large Trader Reporting Systems: Enhanced monitoring of big players.
Algorithmic Audits: Independent stress testing and code reviews.

Chapter 20: Forex Regulations Around the World

Major Players in the Forex Regulation Game

The foreign exchange (Forex) market is a wild beast – it's the world's biggest financial market, open all hours, and trades trillions of dollars daily. With so much money flying around, you'd expect someone to be keeping an eye on things, right? That's where regulatory bodies step in. They're like the referees of the Forex world, making sure everyone plays fair and investors don't get fleeced.

Let's meet some of the big hitters:

The U.S. Powerhouses: NFA and CFTC
America's got two main watchdogs for Forex:
National Futures Association (NFA): Think of them as the industry's self-police. They focus on Forex dealers and brokers, making sure they have enough cash on hand, aren't being shady, etc. (https://www.nfa.futures.org/)
Commodity Futures Trading Commission (CFTC): A government agency, these guys oversee the broader world of futures and options, which includes some Forex stuff. (https://www.cftc.gov/)

UK's Financial Conduct Authority (FCA): The British Bulldog
The FCA is known for its no-nonsense approach. They protect consumers and keep markets running smoothly. If a Forex broker in the UK steps out of line, the FCA isn't afraid to hand out hefty fines or even shut the whole operation down. (https://www.fca.org.uk/)

Australia's ASIC: Keeping Things Fair Down Under

The Australian Securities and Investments Commission (ASIC) doesn't mess around either. They're all about licensing brokers, enforcing rules, and making sure Aussie investors get a fair shake. (https://asic.gov.au/)

Why Should You Care?

These agencies aren't just there to be a pain. They help in a few ways:

Leveling the Playing Field: Regulations make sure smaller investors aren't completely at the mercy of big banks and institutions.
Protecting Your Money: Segregated accounts, minimum capital requirements – these rules aim to keep your investment safe(ish) if a broker goes belly up.
Weeding out the Scammers: While fraudsters still exist, strong regulation makes it much harder for them to operate.

Case Studies: When Things Go Wrong

Even with regulations, things can spiral out of control. Here are a couple of examples:

The Swiss Franc Shockwave (2015): The Swiss National Bank suddenly unpegged the Swiss franc from the euro, causing chaos. Several Forex brokers went bankrupt overnight, proving that even major currencies can bring big surprises.
The "Flash Crash" (2010): In just minutes, the Dow Jones Industrial Average plunged almost 1,000 points. While not strictly Forex-related, it showed how electronic trading can cause wild market swings, which can hurt Forex traders too.

Unusual Details & Quirks

Not All Regulators are Created Equal: Some countries have super-strict rules, others are more laid-back. This creates "regulatory arbitrage" – shady brokers flock to lax jurisdictions to avoid scrutiny.

The Language Barrier: Regulatory rules are often in mind-numbing legalese. Sometimes even brokers don't fully understand what they're supposed to be doing!

Playing Cat and Mouse: Regulators are always playing catch-up with the latest trends and scams in Forex. It's a constant battle.

Remember: Do Your Homework

Just because a broker is regulated, doesn't mean it's 100% trustworthy. Always research a Forex broker thoroughly before handing over your cash.

KYC/AML: The Underbelly of the Forex World

Foreign exchange (forex) trading is a massive, swirling market of currencies. But lurking under those trillions in daily turnover lies the potential for illicit activity. That's where KYC (Know Your Customer) and AML (Anti-Money Laundering) regulations come in, acting like a net to try and snag the bad actors in this global financial sea.

Why Forex is a Magnet for Money Laundering

Anonymity: Forex used to be the Wild West of finance – traders could hide behind screens with minimal identification. This is changing, but loopholes remain.
Cross-border Complexity: Money can zip across countries in seconds, obscuring its origin and making it hard for regulators to track.
Vastness: The sheer volume of forex trades makes it easier for dirty money to blend in, like a single counterfeit bill slipped into a massive stack.

KYC: Turning the Spotlight on Traders

Think of KYC as the forex market's bouncer. Its core principles:

Customer Identification Program (CIP): Forex brokers are obligated to collect and verify proof of identity – think passports, utility bills, etc. No more anonymous trading.
Customer Due Diligence (CDD): This goes a layer deeper. Are you a regular trader or a politically exposed person (PEP)? What's your income source? Brokers need to build a profile to spot risk.

Enhanced Due Diligence (EDD): High-risk clients (think PEPs or those from dodgy countries) get extra scrutiny. More paperwork, more questions.

Real World KYC Messiness

Sounds straightforward, right? Not always. Let's look at some challenges:

Fake Docs: Fraudsters are pros at forging documents. Technology (like AI-powered ID checks) helps, but it's a constant arms race.
Shell Companies: Criminals hide behind layers of businesses, making true ownership a muddy puzzle.
Jurisdictional Juggling: Strict KYC in the UK? A money launderer might just hop over to a lax Caribbean nation.

AML: Following the Money Trail

AML is all about sniffing out suspicious activity. It involves:

Transaction Monitoring: Sophisticated software flags unusual patterns – small deposits suddenly followed by huge transfers, for example.
Suspicious Activity Reports (SARs): Brokers must file SARs to authorities if they smell something fishy.
Sanctions Screening: Clients are cross-checked against lists of sanctioned individuals and countries. Dealing with them is a big no-no.

Case Study: The Forex Broker, the Oligarch, and the
Missing Millions

Scenario: A small forex broker in Cyprus suddenly sees
deposits skyrocket from a Russian businessman known to
be close to Putin.
Red Flags: Client is a PEP, the source of funds is
unclear, transaction patterns are erratic.
Outcome: Broker either fails to file an SAR (risking
hefty fines or worse) or alerts authorities, potentially
disrupting a major money-laundering operation.

The Evolving KYC/AML Landscape

Regulators are constantly tightening the net, but bad
actors adapt too. Here's what the future might hold:

The Blockchain Buzz: Some see blockchain as a
potential AML tool—a transparent, unchangeable ledger
of transactions. It's early days, but the idea is intriguing.
AI Gets Smarter: AI can already analyze vast data sets
for patterns humans would miss. Expect even more
sophisticated algorithms in the years to come.
Global Coordination: Patchwork regulation is a money
launderer's friend. Increased international cooperation is
key to truly choking off illicit flows.

Crucial Note: This is a complex topic; what's legal and
what constitutes a "red flag" varies wildly across
jurisdictions. Brokers need to deeply understand the rules
where they operate.

Sources (Remember, Always Verify!)

Financial Action Task Force (FATF) -
Recommendations on AML: https://www.fatf-
gafi.org/en/home.html
US Treasury – Financial Crimes Enforcement Network
(FinCEN): https://www.fincen.gov/)
FCA (UK) – Regulations on Money Laundering:
https://www.fca.org.uk/firms/financial-crime/money-
laundering-regulations

Leverage Restrictions and Margin Requirements in Forex Regulations

The world of foreign exchange (Forex) is abuzz with the potential for high returns… and equally high risks. To manage this volatility, regulators around the globe impose rules on leverage and margin requirements. Let's explore this regulatory landscape and how it shapes the way traders dance with the Forex market.

Understanding the Tango: Leverage and Margin

Leverage: Think of leverage as a loan your broker gives you. It allows you to control a much larger amount of currency than your actual investment. Like a magnifying glass, leverage amplifies potential profits and losses. Margin: This is your good-faith deposit – your skin in the game. It's expressed as a percentage of the full position size.

Numerical Case Study
Imagine you open a trade worth $100,000 with a leverage of 50:1. This means you only need to put down a margin of $2,000 (100,000/50). If the market moves in your favor by 1%, you gain $1,000, a 50% return on your initial

margin. But if the market moves against you by 1%, you lose that same $1,000 – half of your investment!

The Regulatory Waltz: How Rules Change the Rhythm

Different countries have different attitudes towards risk in the Forex market. Let's look at some major players:

United States: The US takes a relatively conservative stance, limiting leverage to 50:1 on major currency pairs and 20:1 on less common ones. This is designed to protect less experienced traders. [Source: National Futures Association (NFA): https://www.nfa.futures.org/]
European Union: The EU recently tightened its regulations, capping leverage at 30:1 for retail traders on major currency pairs. This aims to curb the excessive risk-taking that was previously possible. [Source: European Securities and Markets Authority (ESMA): https://www.esma.europa.eu/]
Japan: Japan permits leverage of up to 25:1, offering a middle ground between the US and the EU's previous, looser rules. [Source: Financial Services Agency Japan (FSA): https://www.fsa.go.jp/en/]
Emerging Markets: Some countries have even stricter leverage limits, while others may have more relaxed regulations. It's essential to research the specifics for any market you want to trade in.

The Impact: Less Swing, More Sway?

Tighter leverage restrictions have several implications:

Reduced Risk: Lower leverage limits potential losses, potentially making Forex more appealing to risk-averse investors.

Need for Larger Deposits: Traders now need more upfront capital to participate in the same size trades. Subtler Market Moves: Some argue that tighter leverage leads to less volatility in the market, as traders can't take on massive positions with little capital. Others counter that volatility is driven by many factors beyond just leverage.

The Trader's Adaptation

Savvy traders adjust their strategies to thrive within these regulations:

Focusing on Fundamentals: With reduced leverage, technical analysis may not be enough. Traders need a stronger understanding of the economic forces that drive currency values.
Smaller but More Trades: Instead of a few big swings, traders may take more frequent smaller trades seeking to accumulate gains over time.
Tighter Risk Management: Disciplined stop-loss orders and careful position sizing become even more essential to avoid catastrophic losses.

Important Notes:

Regulations are always subject to change. Stay up-to-date on the latest rules in your target markets.
Broker-specific rules may be even stricter than national regulations.

The Forex landscape is a dynamic stage where traders and regulators engage in a constant, intricate performance. Understanding leverage and margin restrictions is key to navigating this exciting but potentially perilous financial arena.

Consumer Protection and Dispute Resolution

The foreign exchange market (Forex) is a behemoth, with trillions of dollars changing hands daily. Its decentralized, global nature creates challenges for consumer protection, particularly for retail traders who may lack financial sophistication. This piece explores how regulations around the world address this, focusing on dispute resolution mechanisms.

The Need for Consumer Protection

Forex trading carries inherent risks:

Volatility: Currency prices fluctuate rapidly, leading to swift gains or losses.
Leverage: Brokers often offer high leverage, magnifying potential profits and losses.
Complexity: Forex products can be intricate, making it difficult for retail investors to fully assess risk.
Scams: The market is, unfortunately, rife with fraudulent brokers and schemes.

Regulatory Patchwork

Consumer protection in Forex is a complex global patchwork. Key regulatory bodies include:

UK: Financial Conduct Authority (FCA)
EU: European Securities and Markets Authority (ESMA)
Japan: Financial Services Agency (FSA)
Australia: Australian Securities and Investments Commission (ASIC)

While general consumer protection principles apply, Forex-specific regulations vary substantially.

Key Areas of Regulation

Broker Licensing: Many jurisdictions mandate that Forex brokers hold licenses and meet certain capital requirements.
Client Fund Segregation: Rules often require brokers to keep client funds separate from their operational funds, offering protection in case of broker bankruptcy.
Marketing Restrictions: Regulators police misleading advertising or exaggerated performance claims.
Leverage Limits: Some jurisdictions cap leverage available to retail traders, aiming to curb excessive risk-taking.

Dispute Resolution: The Critical Gap

While regulations are essential, they're only as good as their enforcement. Dispute resolution is where things get tricky for average traders:
Cross-Border Complexity: When a trader in one country has a dispute with a broker in another, jurisdiction becomes murky.
Cost Barriers: Legal action can be prohibitively expensive, especially for small claims.
Ombudsmen: Some countries offer financial ombudsmen services (FOS in Australia, for example), but their powers may be limited in Forex cases.
Chargebacks: Credit/debit card chargebacks can be a recourse against fraudulent brokers, but success isn't guaranteed.

Case Study: The "Swiss Franc Shock" of 2015

In January 2015, the Swiss National Bank unexpectedly removed its currency peg against the euro. The Swiss franc skyrocketed, causing massive losses for traders (particularly those with leveraged positions). This event highlighted:

Unpredictability of FX: Even seemingly stable currencies can experience seismic shifts.
Broker Bankruptcy: Several brokers went under, leaving clients without recourse to recover losses.

Emerging Trends and Unusual Angles

Social Media's Role: Online forums play an increasing part in flagging scams and coordinating trader efforts to seek redress.
"Whistleblower" Websites: Dedicated platforms allow anonymous reporting of broker misconduct, though the veracity of such information needs careful vetting.
The Rise of Crypto in Forex: Some brokers now accept cryptocurrencies. This raises new regulatory questions about asset classification and volatility.

Sources

CFTC Forex Information: https://www.cftc.gov/LearnAndProtect/AdvisoriesAnd Articles/CFTCFraudAdvisories/index.htm) FCA Forex Regulation Overview: https://www.babypips.com/forexpedia/fca International Organization of Securities Commissions (IOSCO): https://www.iosco.org/)

Important Note: This is a starting point! Regulations change frequently. It's vital to verify information with the specific regulatory bodies before making any investment decisions.

Regional Differences in Taxation of Forex Trading

The foreign exchange (forex) market is a global whirlwind of currency speculation and hedging. While the concepts of forex trading are relatively consistent worldwide, the way governments tax these activities can be wildly different. Understanding these regional quirks is crucial for any trader hoping to maximize profits and stay on the right side of the law.

Taxation Approaches: A Spectrum

Forex as Capital Gains: Many nations, including the United States, treat forex profits as capital gains. This means traders are taxed based on the difference between buying and selling prices, with rates often varying based on how long an asset is held (short-term vs. long-term gains).

Forex as Ordinary Income: Some countries, like the UK for some residents, tax forex profits as ordinary income. This can mean higher tax burdens, as income brackets are often higher than those for capital gains.

Exemptions: There are nations, like Singapore, where forex profits may be entirely tax-exempt under specific circumstances. These havens can be attractive for traders.

The Nuances That Matter

Beyond the broad categories, the devil is in the details of forex taxation:

Trader Status: Are you considered a casual forex trader or a professional? Professional status can unlock deductions for business expenses but might also change your tax category.
Spread Betting: Countries like the UK offer "spread betting" on forex. This can be a tax-efficient way to participate in the market, as winnings are often tax-free.
Carry Trades: Strategies built on interest rate differentials between currencies can face unique tax complications, as some nations may tax interest earned as a separate income source.

Case Studies: The Impact of Taxes

The U.S. Trader: A U.S. citizen making $50,000 in short-term forex gains might be taxed at their ordinary income rate (potentially 25% or higher). The same profits held long-term could be taxed at a lower capital gains rate (potentially 15%).
The Singaporean Advantage: A Singaporean trader, under the right circumstances, might pay zero taxes on forex gains, providing a significant edge over traders in higher-tax jurisdictions.
The U.K. Spread Better: A U.K. resident making £20,000 through spread betting on forex might keep their whole profit tax-free. A standard forex trade with the same gain could be subject to capital gains tax.

Beyond the Basics

Taxation isn't the only regional difference in forex trading. Always consider:

Regulations: Countries have varying degrees of forex market oversight, impacting available brokers and leverage.
Reporting Requirements: How trades are reported to tax authorities varies greatly, affecting your recordkeeping burdens.

Important Notes

Tax laws are complex and change frequently. Never rely solely on general information like this; consult a tax professional.
This draft offers a starting point for exploration, not a comprehensive guide.

Sources

[Investopedia: Forex Taxes]
[FXCM: Taxes on Forex Trading Around the World]
[Government Websites: Seek official tax websites for the countries you're interested in]

Chapter 21: Finding Reliable Brokers and Resources

Evaluating Forex Brokers

The world of forex trading is a beast of its own – thrilling, lucrative, but riddled with potential pitfalls. One of the first and most important steps for a trader is finding a reliable broker. But how do you cut through the marketing fluff and get to the heart of what a broker truly offers? Let's dive in!

1. Regulation: The Non-Negotiable

Think of regulation like a referee in a boxing ring – it ensures fair play. Always choose a broker regulated by a top-tier authority. Some reputable ones include:

Financial Conduct Authority (FCA) - UK: Known for strict standards (https://www.fca.org.uk/)
Australian Securities and Investments Commission (ASIC) - Australia: (https://asic.gov.au/)
Commodity Futures Trading Commission (CFTC) and National Futures Association (NFA) - USA: (https://www.cftc.gov/) and (https://www.nfa.futures.org/)

Regulation isn't foolproof, but it dramatically reduces risks like fraudulent activity and protects your funds.

2. Spreads: The Hidden Cost

The spread is the difference between a currency pair's buy and sell price. It's essentially the broker's commission.

Look for brokers with consistently tight spreads on the pairs you trade most.

Case Study: Broker A offers a EUR/USD spread of 1.5 pips, while Broker B offers 0.8 pips. Over 100 trades on a standard lot, that's a potential difference of $700 in costs!

3. Platforms: Your Trading Cockpit

A good trading platform is intuitive, packed with analysis tools, and stable. MetaTrader 4/5 are industry favorites, but many brokers offer proprietary platforms worth exploring.

Pro Tip: Test platforms with demo accounts before committing real funds.

4. Customer Service: Your Lifeline

The forex market never sleeps, so ideally, neither should your broker's support. 24/7 availability, multiple contact channels (phone, email, live chat), and quick response times are signs of a quality broker.

Case Study: Imagine your open position hits its stop-loss unexpectedly overnight. Speedy customer service could mean the difference between a minor loss and a blown account.

Beyond the Basics: Some Unusual Angles

Account Types: Many brokers offer tiered account structures. Higher tiers might offer better spreads but have hefty minimum deposits. Always weigh the potential benefits against your starting capital.

Slippage: This occurs when your order gets filled at a worse price than you intended, often during high volatility. Ask brokers about their slippage policies.
Community: Some brokers have active forums or social media channels. This can be great for learning and networking, especially as a beginner.

Finding Reliable Resources

Evaluating brokers takes legwork. Here are some trustworthy sources:

Regulatory Websites: Check if a broker is registered and view any disciplinary history.
ForexPeaceArmy (https://www.forexpeacearmy.com/): A crowd-sourced review platform with trader experiences. Take reviews with a grain of salt, but it can be a good starting point.
Finance Blogs/YouTube Channels: Some offer in-depth broker analyses and comparisons

Important Note: The best forex broker for you depends entirely on your individual needs and style. Some traders prioritize razor-thin spreads, others want advanced educational resources.

Let's Get Numerical – A Hypothetical Scenario

Imagine you're a beginner trader with $2,000 starting capital, focusing on major currency pairs. You want:

*Top-tier regulation

Competitive spreads
A user-friendly platform
Decent customer support

After research, you narrow it down to Broker A and Broker B. A deep dive into their offerings and reviews could help you decide.

Remember, broker choice is an ongoing process. As your skills and capital grow, you might need different features or switch brokers altogether. Stay informed and make choices that empower your trading journey!

Resources for learning

Understanding Forex: The Building Blocks

Before diving into brokers, a solid grasp of forex is crucial. Here's your educational toolkit:

Books That Lay the Foundation:
"Currency Trading for Dummies" (Kathleen Brooks, Brian Dolan): A beginner-friendly breakdown of forex fundamentals. ([Link to Amazon or similar retailer]).
"Japanese Candlestick Charting Techniques" (Steve Nison): Delve into candlestick patterns, a cornerstone of technical analysis. ([Link to Amazon or similar retailer]).

Websites for Real-Time Learning:
Babypips.com: Their free "School of Pipsology" is an industry-recognized forex course packed with lessons and quizzes. (https://www.babypips.com/)
Investopedia: Look up forex-specific terminology or concepts for bite-sized, reliable explanations (https://www.investopedia.com/).
DailyFX: Offers market analysis, news, and educational webinars (https://www.dailyfx.com/).

Forums: The Pulse of the Community

Forex Factory: A hub for traders to discuss strategies, share indicators, and get insights from market sentiment (https://www.forexfactory.com/).
Reddit's Forex Subreddit (r/Forex): A diverse pool of traders with varying experience levels ([invalid URL removed]). Note: Exercise caution and cross-check information from forums.

Finding the Right Broker: Your Trading Partner

Selecting a broker isn't a one-size-fits-all decision. Consider these factors:

Regulation: The Backbone of Trust
Look for brokers regulated by top-tier authorities like the FCA (UK), ASIC (Australia), or CySec (EU).
[invalid URL removed]: This site has detailed broker reviews and a "scam watch" section for added safety ([invalid URL removed]).
Spreads and Commissions: The Cost of Doing Business
Compare the typical "spread" (the difference between buy and sell prices) offered by different brokers. Some brokers charge commission per trade, others have it factored into the spread. Analyze which model suits your trading style.
Trading Platform: Your Cockpit
Most brokers offer MetaTrader 4/5, industry-standard platforms with charting tools and customization. Some have proprietary platforms, check reviews for user-friendliness.
Account Types: Tailored to Your Needs
Many brokers offer "micro" or "cent" accounts for beginners with lower minimum deposits.

Consider account leverage limits, especially if you're starting out.

Numerical Case Study: The Impact of Spreads

Let's see how spreads affect your trading:

Scenario: You trade 1 standard lot (100,000 units) of EUR/USD.
Broker A: Spread of 1 pip
Broker B: Spread of 3 pips

A pip for EUR/USD is roughly $10. This means:

Broker A's Cost: 1 pip * $10/pip = $10 cost per trade
Broker B's Cost 3 pips * $10/pip = $30 cost per trade

This $20 difference per trade can significantly impact your profitability, especially if you trade frequently.

Extra Tips for a Savvy Search:

Words of Caution: Avoid resources promising "get rich quick" with forex; trading carries inherent risks.
Demo Accounts: Your Risk-Free Trial: Most brokers offer demo accounts to practice trading strategies before committing real funds.
Consider reaching out to a reputable financial advisor with FX experience, especially if you'll be investing significant amounts.

Keeping Up with Market News and Analysis

Staying on top of forex news isn't just about reading headlines; it's about understanding the context and potential impacts.

Unusual News Sources: Major outlets (Reuters, Bloomberg) are essential, but consider:
Central Bank Websites: Get info straight from the horse's mouth – economic outlooks, interest rate decisions [invalid URL removed] example).
Niche Industry Blogs: These can offer specific analysis on currency pairs or trading strategies.
Economic Calendars: These schedules of data releases are vital, but don't just look at the numbers:
"Whisper Numbers": These are the market's expectations, often more important than the official data (https://www.investopedia.com/terms/w/whispernumber.asp).
Reaction, Not Just Release: Big surprise relative to expectations? That drives volatility and trading opportunity.

Case Study (Unusual News Impact):

Let's say the website of the Reserve Bank of Australia drops a surprise hint about an upcoming rate hike. Traders weren't expecting this, so it's a big deal.

Generic Take: "AUD likely to strengthen based on RBA statement."

Finding Reliable Brokers and Resources
This is where reputation and regulation matter more than flashy ads. Think like an investigator!

It's Not Just About Reviews:

Regulator Check: Is your broker properly licensed in your region? (Examples: ASIC in Australia, FCA in the UK https://asic.gov.au/ https://www.fca.org.uk/)

Transparency Test: Are spreads and fees clearly explained upfront? Avoid brokers with hidden costs.

Unusual Resource: Community Forums

Not for Stock Tips: But to get a feel for the broker's reputation, customer service, platform quirks, etc.

Look for Specifics, Not Hype: "XYZ broker withdrawal was slow" is more useful than "XYZ broker is the BEST!"

Case Study (Red Flags):

You find a broker with incredible spreads and a slick website, but they're licensed in a country you've never heard of.

Generic Take: "This broker seems too good to be true."

Smarter Take: "I need more info. Lack of regulation in [country] means less protection if things go wrong. Balancing risk vs. reward is key."

Advanced AI for Forex

This gets exciting, but remember: AI is a tool, not a magic money machine.

Sentiment Analysis:

News Scouring: AI can find subtle shifts in market mood faster than you can read articles.

Social Media Too: But beware, online chatter isn't always reliable.

Pattern Recognition Beyond Charts:

AI might spot correlations between economic data, news events, and price action that humans miss.
The Catch: Correlation isn't causation. This is a starting point, not a finished strategy.

Case Study (AI Sentiment Shift):

Your AI tool flags increasing negativity in news about the Eurozone economy. Pair this with technical analysis of EUR/USD.

Generic Take: "EUR/USD might be in for a downtrend."
Smarter Take: "Negative sentiment aligns with a bearish breakout pattern on EUR/USD. Considering short positions, but will watch for any policy surprises from the European Central Bank."

Key Points:

Unique = Specific + Context Not just fancy words, but understanding the WHY behind market moves.
Your Job is the Human Touch: AI finds data, you provide the insight that makes it tradable.

Understanding Forex Signals

The Basics: Signal providers in forex offer trade recommendations (buy/sell, entry/exit points). These can be automated (algorithmic) or based on human analysis. Not a Magic Bullet: Signals are tools, not guaranteed profit. Success still hinges on your risk management, market understanding, and chosen broker.

Types of Signals:

Technical: Derived from chart patterns, indicators, etc.

Fundamental: Based on economic news, central bank events

Hybrid: A mix of both technical and fundamental factors

Spotting Reliable Signal Providers (the Tricky Part!)

Here's where your "unusual word choices" request comes in. Due to the unregulated nature of this space, separating the wheat from the chaff is crucial.

Verified Track Record: Don't fall for cherry-picked results. Look for independently audited performance with a decent history (years, not months). Sites like Myfxbook can help.

Transparency of Method: Vague strategies are a red flag. Good providers outline their approach (technical setups, news factors they follow, etc.)

Realistic Expectations: Outrageous win rates (>90%) scream scam. The market is dynamic; even the pros have losing trades.

Community & Reviews: Scour forums, but beware of fake testimonials. Sites like Trustpilot may be more reliable, though not foolproof.

The "Smell Test": If the claims seem too good, your gut is probably right.

Case Study (Numerical-ish): The Power of Backtesting

Let's say you find a provider focused on EUR/USD with:

70% claimed win-rate over 2 years
Average risk-reward ratio of 1:2 (i.e., twice the
potential profit vs. loss)

Don't just take their word for it. Backtest using historical
data on a platform like TradingView. This gives you a
controlled reality-check.

Caveats: Even good past performance is no guarantee of
the future. Slippage (real-world execution prices vs. ideal
signals) also distorts results.

Extra Dimension: The Broker Factor

Even the best signals won't help with an awful broker.
Look for:

Regulation: Reputable bodies like the FCA (UK), ASIC
(Australia), etc. are a safer bet.
Spreads: These are transaction costs. The tighter, the
better, especially if you scalp based on signals.
Execution Speed: Signals, especially fast ones, need
minimal delay in order placement.
Resources: Does the broker offer news feeds,
economic calendars, etc., to complement the signals?

Unusual Angles to Consider

Psychology of Following Signals: Can you handle handing your decision-making to someone else? This takes discipline.

The 'Tail Risk' Signal Providers Ignore: News events, black swan scenarios, etc. These can blow up accounts, so always have your own stop-losses in place.

Niche is Nice: Some providers excel in specific pairs or within certain market hours (London open, etc.). Consider this for alignment with your style.

Sources (a starting point, not exhaustive)

Myfxbook: https://www.myfxbook.com/
Forex Peace Army (Forums): [invalid URL removed]
Trustpilot: [invalid URL removed]

Important Disclaimer: I'm an AI, not a financial advisor. This is intended for educational exploration, not as a direct recommendation for any specific provider or broker.

9 783384 451347